Planning Your Rare Coin Retirement

How to Select a $10,000 Rare Coin Portfolio Full of Growth Potential

David L. Ganz

Bonus Books, Inc., Chicago

For Kathy,
whom I hope to share my rare coin retirement with,
with all my love.

02   01   00   99   98   5   4   3   2   1

Library of Congress Cataloging-in-Publication Data

Ganz, David L.
    Planning your rare coin retirement / by David L. Ganz.
      p.   cm.
    Includes index.
    ISBN 1-56625-098-6 (alk. paper)
    1. Coins, American—Collectors and collecting—Handbooks, manuals,
etc. 2. Coins as an investment—Handbooks, manuals, etc.
    3. Retirement—United States—Planning—Handbooks, manuals, etc.
I. Title.
CJ1832.G36   1998
332.63—dc21   98-17193
                                                    CIP

Bonus Books, Inc.
160 East Illinois Street
Chicago, Illinois 60611

Printed in the United States of America

Contents

Acknowledgments   v

Preface   ix

Planning Your Rare Coin Retirement: Measure Gains & Losses through
   the Years   1

What You Need to Know about Coin Grading for Your Rare Coin
   Portfolio Retirement Plan   9

Where to Purchase Coins for Your Rare Coin Retirement   25

A Chart of Possibilities for Your Rare Coin Portfolio   27

Carson City Silver Dollars   35

Indian Head Cents 1900–1909   43

1997 Platinum Tenth of an Ounce Bullion Coin   47

Thomas Jefferson Commemorative Dollar   51

Jefferson Nickel 1938–1965   55

Eisenhower Dollars 1971–1978   59

Complete Set of Kennedy Half Dollars 1964-1996   63

1989-D Congressional Half Dollar   67

1994 American Numismatic Association Commemorative Platinum Coin
   (Turks & Caicos)   71

Lincoln Cent Collection 1934–1958   75

Lincoln Memorial Cent 1959–1997   79

1993 Madison 50¢ Commemorative   83

1903-O Morgan Silver Dollar   87

Roosevelt Dime Set 1946–1997   91

Roosevelt Dimes 1965–1997   95

1881–S Morgan Silver Dollar   99

1970–D Kennedy Half Dollar   103

1970–S Kennedy Half Dollar   107

Washington Quarters 1941–1964   111

Washington Quarters 1965–1997   115

1904–O Silver Dollar   119

Isle of Man 1/25 Ounce Gold Crown   123

U.S. Proof Set Collection 1950–1997   127

1988-W Olympic $5 Gold Coin   131

Gem Proof Silver Eagle 1986–1996   135

1991 Quarter Ounce $10 Gold American Eagle   139

Five Dollar Gold Pieces   143

Susan B. Anthony Dollar Set 1979–1981   149

Vietnam War Memorial Commemorative Dollar   153

1995 Double Die Lincoln Cent   157

Uncirculated Barber Dime   161

Classic U.S. Commemorative Coins   165

Modern Commemorative Coins   171

Uncirculated Peace Dollars   187

Foreign Gold Coins   193

Platinum Coins for Your Rare Coin Retirement   207

The Rarest of Earth Metals for Your Rare Coin Retirement   217

Acknowledgments

In 1982, I was asked to write "How to Plan Your Rare Coin Retirement," which appeared in the thirty-fifth edition of *A Guidebook of United States Coins*, commonly called the "Red Book" prepared by Richard S. Yeoman, and edited by Kenneth E. Bressett. The article itself arose from an analysis that appeared in a publication of the Federal Reserve Bank of Boston, entitled the *New England Economic Review*. This 1978 publication compared stocks, bonds and other security-like instruments with tangible assets for the first time.

I first learned of the *New England Economic Review* as a student at Georgetown University when I used the Joseph Lauinger Memorial Library to discover the various economic publications of the Federal Reserve banks that were available, at that time free of charge, to any interested student or other person with an abiding interest in an otherwise dismal science.

After writing about the Salomon Brothers review and forecast of collectibles for the "Red Book," I began to do an annual report on it for *COINage* magazine at the request of Jim Miller, the publisher. I also wrote about it on a fairly regular basis for *Coin World*, where my column "Backgrounder" and its various derivatives ran for nearly twenty years, and in *Coins* magazine, where my column "Coin Market Perspective" ran for a decade.

Starting in 1969, my "Under the Glass" column appeared in *Numismatic News*, where it ran until 1976 and where it has since appeared after a twenty-year hiatus. Throughout, I covered the coin market in a variety of roles and positions, first as an observer, second as a columnist, and third as a reporter covering auction developments. I was also an active buyer. It is from this knowledge and experience that I have gained the ability to analyze the market and to pick the coins that I have included in the rare coin retirement portfolio.

My first acknowledgments, therefore, are appropriately due to the publishers of *Numismatic News* and *Coins* magazine (Krause Publications); to Miller Magazines, whose monthly *COINage* magazine remains a joy to write twenty-five years after I first began to cover the coin market, and to *Coin World*, (Amos Press), where I wrote so many articles about coin auctions and coin prices through the years.

Thanks next must go to my agent, Scott Travers, who suggested that there must be an additional book in me besides *The World of Coins and Coin Collecting*, which Bonus Books published in a third, revised edition earlier this year. (The first edition of the book was published in 1980).

Scott and I talked about *Planning Your Rare Coin Retirement*, and I thought it would be catchy and kind of neat to have 100 coins at $100 or a $10,000 portfolio, and he agreed. We have since modified the concept to allow for coins that sell for a bit over, and some for a bit under $100, but the overall goal of a $10,000 portfolio, or multiple portfolios constructed the same way, starts there. I thank him for his encouragement.

Illustrating any coin book is never an easy task, but it was made much easier when Bowers and Merena Galleries (and Q. David Bowers in particular) agreed to furnish photographs. Other photographs in the book come from Stack's Rare Coins (Harvey Stack), Heritage Rare Coins (Jim Halperin and Steve Ivy) and David W. Akers, Incorporated (David W. Akers) together with Superior Galleries (Ira Goldberg).

The contribution of the photography department of Bowers and Merena Galleries in agreeing to supply photos of modern coins not always easily available is deeply appreciated.

I would be remiss if I did not thank my wife, Kathy, for her substantial assistance in helping to organize the manuscript, and in serving as my typist. This is the first book I have not typed entirely on my own, and I must tell you, it is a pleasure to have her help. Word processing on a computer is certainly easier than typing on an IBM Selectric, as *The World of Coins and Coin Collecting* was, but it is still time consuming. In no small measure, this book has been finished in timely fashion because of Kathy's persistence. In addition to being a typist, she also had the first edit, and made me explain things that, to me, seemed self-explanatory. After I did that, her observation was that the book would be better if the explanation was incorporated. I did so on many occasions. She would want me to thank her assistant, Oreo Cookie, our cat, for all her help in sorting the pages as they came out of the printer and for supplying moral support and comic relief to both of us.

My three children, Scott, Elyse and Pamela are also owed a giant "thanks" for putting up with those days and evenings when Dad was on the computer, and they couldn't use it to chat on line.

Finally, though I have been a writer and a reporter for more than a quarter century, for the past twenty years I have also been a practicing lawyer with the New York City law firm of Ganz, Hollinger & Towe, and the Fair Lawn, N.J. firm of Ganz & Sivin, P.A. My thanks to my partners, Jerrietta R. Hollinger, and Teri Towe, for their encouragement with this project, and with my involvement in all aspects of the coin industry.

Preface

Here's the premise: a rare coin portfolio designed to plan for your rare coin retirement, assembled at a total cost of no more than $10,000. That boils down to $100 per coin and a surprising number of possibilities.

That doesn't mean that $100 is an absolute, or a ceiling, because there are actually coins for $49 that are good buys for inclusion in the portfolio, and that gives us the possibility of purchasing a $151 coin.

The 100 coins for $10,000 is not an elusive goal, but one that is affordable to most collectors over some period of time. Surveys from various hobby periodicals and numismatic organizations, show that the typical coin purchaser spends $2,500 per year on his or her hobby. This is for new coins acquired directly from the various minting agencies as well as older coins acquired from dealers.

The average age of coin purchasers is about fifty-five, so in order to take advantage of an appropriate rare coin retirement program, coins included in the portfolio should be those that can be accumulated either now or over a period of three to four years (consistent with the spending patterns). Thus, the items that are in this book are available for purchase now or within the next three to four years. If you begin buying the coins for your portfolio when you are fifty-five years old, by age fifty-nine, your rare coin retirement portfolio could be complete. The portfolio is to be held for twelve years, until by law, if it is really a pension, it must be liquidated.

Of course, this is a hypothetical portfolio. With several exceptions, principally bullion coinage of the United States and foreign countries, rare coins are not allowed in individual retirement accounts (IRAs). Section 408(m) of the Internal Revenue Code of 1954, as amended, took that right away effective August, 1981, although rare coins are permitted in self-directed plans where there is an independent trustee who agrees that they are a useful investment. (The Internal Revenue Code revision in 1986 continued this practice.)

In picking the items for this model portfolio, the focus has been on coins that are interesting, and that have a significant upside in potential value. If you like the idea enough to double it, there are at least two portfolios worth of coins included in this book, one of which is entirely composed of gold and platinum coins, the other of which is a mixture of gold, platinum, silver, and copper coinage from around the world (though coins of the United States predominate).

The prices of the coins must be documentable. There's not much point in telling you to acquire an 1804 silver dollar for $100 when the real price is $1.8 million. Thus, the line of demarcation is drawn based on an advertisement in a periodical, an auction price, or even a price in a standard catalogue for a particular type or series. As of the summer of 1997, each coin listed in this book could be purchased at or around the price stated.

Most of the coins that are found in the pages that follow have widespread availability through coin dealers, or from the issuing authority (the mint that struck them or its agents). There are "new issues" that are included as well as older ones. Coins that can be found in circulation are included, as are coins that can only be obtained, at least initially, from a government mint.

This is a portfolio that you can track on an annual basis, and that will be tracked in various hobby periodicals over the next dozen years. You will be able to see your investment grow and compare it to returns in the equities market, precious metal sales and even consumer prices.

If you decide to compile a portfolio of rare coins based on the suggestions in this book some important caveats are in order: The coins that have been chosen here are recommended based on the author's experience, past performance, and speculative advice. Rare coin investment is not for the timid, because there are no guarantees. A coin may go up in value, down in value or stay the same, and if it goes down or stays the same over a period of a dozen years, the investor is the ultimate loser. Coins have had their ups and downs through the years, and the model portfolio that follows will probably prove to be no exception to this.

Examine this book and the coins listed in it carefully and satisfy yourself that this is the right investment for you. Don't look for the proverbial bargain at a price substantially lower than those quoted in the book because, as the late Lee F. Hewitt, publisher of *Numismatic Scrapbook* once said, "There is no Santa Claus in numismatics."

When purchasing coins for investment purposes, condition counts. If a coin is graded uncirculated but isn't, it's true value in the market place will be substantially less than an uncirculated item. If a coin is graded MS-65 (a very superior grade of uncirculated, known as "gem") but is in fact MS-64 (a very nice coin, but of a lesser quality called "choice uncirculated") the difference in price can be geometric. Coin grading is essentially a matter of opinion. However, there are a number of reliable third-party grading services who offer their opinion as to the grade or state of preservation of a coin for a fee. Generally speaking, it is wise to purchase the highest grade coin that you can for the money that you can afford.

Many other coins not included in this book merit consideration for someone planning their rare coin retirement. The anecdotal tales of individuals who have made purchases of rare coins and were handsomely rewarded years later, is astonishing. A New York lawyer, Harold Bareford, is known to have purchased approximately $13,000 in rare coins between 1945 and 1954. His collection was sold at public auction by Stack's, a well-known rare coin auctioneer in New York City, in October, 1978. The collection brought a price of more than 1 million dollars.

Starting in 1997, David W. Akers, Inc., sold off the accumulated collection of John Jay Pittman, who collected coins from 1943 until his death in 1996. The bulk of the collection, however, was assembled between 1943 and 1961, though intermittent purchases were made in later years. Pittman, a chemical engineer with Eastman Kodak Company, in Rochester, New York, made his rare coin purchases by discovering "sleepers," or coins whose appeal had not yet been universally discovered. Except for his purchases at the Palace Collection auction sale in Cairo in 1954 (when the Egyptian government nationalized the collection of King Farouk and had Sotheby's sell it), virtually all of Pittman's purchases were individual coins. Over the course of his collecting lifetime, based solely on discretionary income from his job as an engineer, he amassed a coin collection that experts believe will be worth more than $30 million when the sale is finally completed.

Rare coins are not like stocks. It's difficult to track them on a daily basis, except for those whose dominant component is their bullion content or precious metal worth. If that's the kind of investment you want to make so that you can see how your value progresses on a daily basis rare coins probably are not for you.

Most likely, in order to find the worth of your product, you'll either be buying a subscription to a periodical that lists such information (and putting the data onto a spreadsheet yourself), or purchasing a computer program and data base that lists the value of the items you have included in your rare coin retirement collection.

Two additional caveats: Don't invest more than you are capable of losing, and don't shy away from negotiating over the price of any item you want to acquire. It's a free marketplace, and there is no uniformity in pricing. Different vendors will sell the identical item at widely disparate prices. Finally, this is an investment vehicle that is not well regulated by the government. Consumer protection regulations in some states are applicable, but as activities of the Federal Trade Commission have shown, it is a field that can attract the unscrupulous, eager to sell an inferior product to an unsuspecting, gullible (but very interested) public.

Coins have been a good investment for more than fifty years, and even in this era of record highs of the Dow Jones Industrial Average and stock prices, there's still a place for rare coins in your investment portfolio.

This book will show you that it is possible to plan your coin retirement, and to do it with a portfolio of 100 coins whose average cost is $100, and in the process, introduce you to the fabulous world of coin collecting.

Planning Your
Rare Coin Retirement

Measuring Rare Coin Gains
and Losses through the Years

You can plan your rare coin retirement starting today. Like any other investment, when you collect coins for investment purposes it is essential that you have the tools to monitor the gains and losses in the coin market. Rare coins are a valid medium, though largely an unregulated one. The result is that it is essential for everyone whose goal is to watch their investment with a mind to take appropriate action when necessary, to have a means of comparison—a yardstick with which to measure their investment's gains and losses. In addition, without these tools it would be very difficult to explain just how you can retire with rare coins. One of these tools is a market basket of rare coins, which, like another market basket called the Dow Jones Industrial Index, measures the trends of a specific product. In the case of the Dow Jones Industrial Index, the market basket is made up of the stocks of large industrial corporations, but our market basket measures the rare coin market. Both were designed as a research tool to be used by the consumer to get a general picture of the financial health of their respective marketplaces.

Investors in stocks have been tracking their investment portfolios with the Dow Jones Industrial Average for over one hundred years. The Dow measures the average loss or gain of thirty representative large, American, industrial corporations. The thirty stocks that make up this index are a "market basket." The make-up of the market basket may change over time: whenever one corporation ceases to be representative of large industrial corporations as a whole. For example, in 1928, AT&T was dropped from the Index, and IBM was added. Just nine years later, IBM's fast growth made it no longer representative of large industry as a whole, so it was dropped and AT&T was returned to the Index.

Today the Dow Jones Industrial Index includes a portfolio of stock from AT&T, IBM, American Express, Boeing, Coca Cola, Disney, DuPont, Kodak, Exxon, General Electric, General Motors, 3M, Proctor and Gamble, Sears Roebuck and sixteen others. What the Dow Jones Industrial Average measures for the investor every day is the price fluctuation of a portfolio of all thirty stocks (which have been weighted to account for stock splits). Though an investor might not have all thirty stocks, or may have a stock from a large industrial corporation, but one that is not part of the market basket of the Dow, that investor can assume with some certainty that his or her stock will have similar fluctuations as those that are chosen to represent Industry as a whole. The Index will not predict the specific gains or losses of a particular stock, what the Index will do is give an investor an idea of the likely performance of any large industrial corporation's stock every day.

What the Index also allows the investor to do is track the growth of these stocks over time. Because the Dow Jones Industrial Average has been tracking the price fluctuations of its market basket for over one hundred years, an investor can look back and see what kind of return can be expected over years, or even decades. Though the make-up of the market basket may have changed over the years, the corporations are still representative of Industry as a whole. So, if over the last twenty-five years, the portfolio of stock that makes up the Dow Jones Industrial Index has grown 50 percent in value, you could predict with some degree of certainty that the same market basket has a good chance of continuing to grow at this rate over the next twenty-five years. There is some risk, of course, in making this prediction. There is no guarranty that your twenty-five year investment in the Dow Jones Industrial Index will pay off at the same rate, but there is at least some evidence to suggest that it might, and that is about as certain as things get in the world of investment.

Rare coins, however do not have a daily index with which to follow your rare coin retirement investment. An index similar to the Dow Jones Industrial Index was assembled in 1978 and was administered until 1990 on behalf of Salomon Brothers by Stack's Rare Coins, a New York City coin dealership that advertises itself as America's "oldest and largest" rare coin dealer. Salomon Brothers tracked rare coins and other investment vehicles and collectibles such as rare stamps, Chinese ceramics, farmland, Old Masters, Treasury bills, stocks, bonds, gold and diamonds by having experts in each field compile a representative market basket of each item. Like the Dow Jones Industrial Index, which neither represents all publicly held companies, nor even all significant stocks that trade on the exchange, Salomon Brothers portfolio of rare coins does not represent all rare coins, or even the most popular rare coins. It is a market basket that is broadly representative of the rare coin market as a whole, and to that extent, its trendline represents what the market actually does.

The Salomon Brother's survey for rare coins ran only from 1978 through 1990, but can be tracked backwards using auction and other sales records. The coins for the index were chosen by experts in the field as being coins that might be found in a broad, general collection of rare coins. "We chose these coins because they were representative of the kind of coins that were widely collected," said Harvey Stack in an early interview. The Salomon Brothers' coin portfolio consisted of twenty coins that were chosen as being representative of a type set of copper and silver coinage, most of which was in choice uncirculated condition (MS–60). No gold coins were included because Salomon Brothers believed that changes in the gold market would also affect the price of gold coins and cause unnatural price fluctuations.

Just as the market basket of the Dow Index changes from time to time so too did the Stacks list. When it chose the coins to be included in the portfolio, Stacks anticipated that it might be difficult to accurately price all of the coins. There were handy substitutes of comparable quality and mintage that could be used instead. For example, an 1866 dime with a mintage of 8,725 could be compared with 1865 dime with a mintage of 10,500, or even the 1863 dime with a mintage of 14,460. Obviously, these coins are not identical, but they are similar enough in year and mintage to be good approximations of the price of the coin if a current price is not available.

The Salomon Brothers list of rare coins includes a 1794 half cent (a scarce copper coin with a mintage of about 82,000 pieces), an 1873 tuppence (struck only as a proof; some 1,100 pieces are known), an 1866 nickel (mintage 14 million), an 1862 silver three cent piece (mintage 362,000) an 1862 half dime (mintage 1.4 milllion), an 1807 bust dime (mintage 165,000) an 1866 Liberty seated dime (mintage, 8,725), an 1876 20-cent piece (mintage 15,900), an 1873 quarter (mintage 1.2 million), an 1896 quarter (mintage 3.8 million), a 1916 Liberty standing quarter (mintage, 52,000), an 1815 dollar (mintage, 47,000), an 1834 half-dollar (mintage, 6.4 million pieces), 1855–O Liberty seated half-dollar (mintage, 3.6 million), a 1921 Walking Liberty (mintage 246,000), a 1795 Draped Bust dollar (mintage, 42,738), an 1847 Seated Liberty dollar (mintage, 140,000), 1881 trade dollar (mintage, 960 proofs), an 1884–S Morgan dollar (mintage 3.2 million), and a 1928 Hawaiian Commemorative half dollar (mintage, about 10,000). When it chose the coins for the portfolio, Stack's anticipated that it might be difficult to accurately price all of the coins, but there were handy substitutes of comparable quality and mintage that could be used instead. For example, an 1834 half-dollar could be substituted for the 1836, as could the 1833. Though their mintages are different, availability and price are practically the same.

If this market basket had been purchased in 1945, it would have cost about $430. Considering that lawyers were paid $31 a week to work on Wall Street that year, the sum is not inconsequential. By 1955, the portfolio had nearly doubled in cost to $781, and today it would cost about $75,000 to purchase this portfolio. This market basket has grown at a rate of about 12 percent a year over the last fifty years, compared with an 8.98 percent growth rate for the Dow Jones. In fact, compare the market basket of rare coins to the Consumer Price Index, the Dow Jones Industrial average, high-grade municipal bonds (5.7 percent), U.S. government long-term bonds (6.5 percent), and the prices of gold and silver and you will find that rare coins have out-performed all of these as well as all collectibles except Chinese ceramics (19.2 percent) and gold bullion (16.3 percent) over the last fifty years (see following figures). What can be seen from the following graphs is a vibrant market for rare coins that has continued to grow—at times far faster than the equities market or other more traditional investment vehicles.

What is also evident from these graphs is that though rare coins are a valid long-term investment vehicle, they have significant short-term voltality, which means that coins have a higher annual return when they are kept for a longer, rather than a shorter period of time. In addition, because of the volatility of the rare coin market, these other investments require minimal risk, while rare coins require investors to take significantly more. Not every year is a winner for any investment, whether it is rare coins, gold, silver, farmland, Treasury bills, or stocks. This is one of the reasons that it is so important that an investor understand the indices like the Dow Jones and the Salomon Brother's. Investments, particularly those investments to be used for retirement, must be measued over the long-term because these funds are not going to be used in a year; they are going to be used ten, twenty, fifty years. It is essential that the investor have an idea how his or her investment will perform over this time period.

The following graphs show the performance of the Salomon Brothers portfolio compared with the Dow Jones Industrial Average, and other investment vehicles and indices over the last fifty years. The Salomon Brothers index did not exist fifty years ago, but the coins did, and their prices are a matter of historical record. The *Old Wayte Raymond Standard Catalogues* prove the validity of the pricing, which can also be examined in *A Guide Book of United States Coins* (the "Red Book"), in advertisements in *The Numismatist* and other periodicals, and in auction records of leading dealers of the day. The graphs prepared by me use the market basket of twenty rare coins originally found on the Salomon Brothers portfolio. The gains and losses recorded on these graphs will differ slightly from the actual percentages and rates of return found in the Salomon Brothers examination because the method of compiling prices for this book differs from the raw auction data used in the compilation of the Salomon Brothers review.

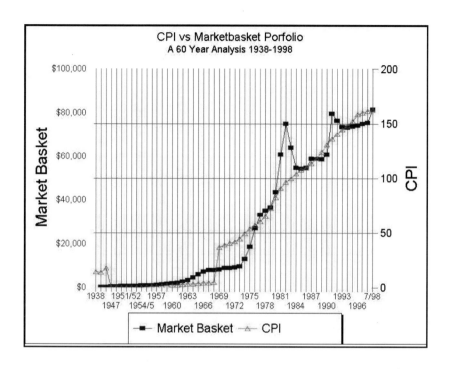

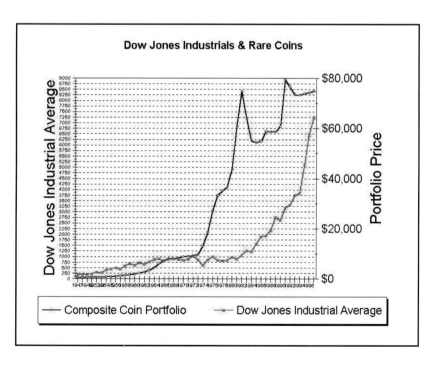

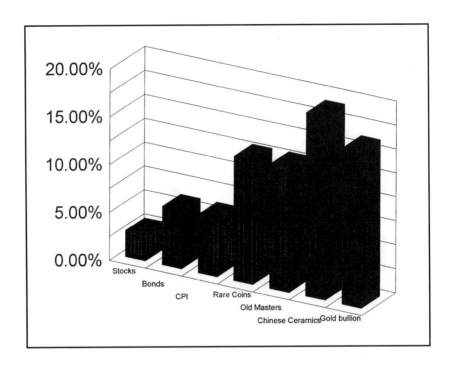

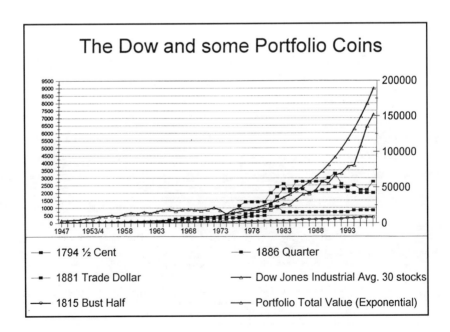

What You Need to Know about Coin Grading for Your Rare Coin Portfolio Retirement Plan

Grading is an attempt to quantify and describe the various states of preservation (or condition) that a coin may be in—it is a means of describing a coin's quality. You need to have some knowledge about this if you want to effectively plan your rare coin retirement.

Coin grades can be described in one of two ways: either using adjectives or numbers. Sometimes, a combination of the two methods is used. The importance of grade manifests itself in the price of an item, for all things being equal, a coin of a higher grade will sell for more than a coin of a lesser grade. As Dr. Richard Doty noted in *The Macmillan Encyclopedic Dictionary of Numismatics* (1982), "along with rarity and demand, [grades] . . . establish the buying and selling prices for coins, tokens, paper money, etc."

A Brief History of Grading

Adjectival grading has gone on since the first coin collector sought a "better" specimen for his or her collection. You can invent or utilize your own adjectives (such as "awful," or "very worn") and as long as you are consistent, it may well serve your purpose. However, if you want to communicate your grade to another collector, or to someone who buys or sells coins, it is vital to use the vernacular of those in the trade.

There are certain adjectives, or descriptive words, that are universally utilized to describe the grade of a coin when the person describing the piece is either a collector or a dealer. These adjectives remain a viable means of describing a coin, and usually incorporate words as follows: poor, fair, good, very good, fine, very fine, extra fine, about uncirculated, uncirculated. Proof (a method of manufacture, not really a grade) can itself be subdivided. Sometimes "plus" or "minus" is utilized; other times "choice" or "premium quality" or some similar word is also added.

Systematic numerical grading began with the 1948 publication by Dr. William Sheldon of *A Penny Whimsy* (also known as *Early American Cents* 1793–1814), which attempted to quantify as well as qualify grading of large cents. The numerical descriptions were later given a verbal explanation, which came to be used to describe all coins of a particular grading description.

Abe Kosoff, a widely respected dealer active from about 1937 into the 1970's wrote in his *Coin World* column of April 25, 1973: "Application of the numeral system is an attempt to apply an exact or mathematical standard to the process of grading coins . . ." Kosoff was correct. It was an *attempt*, which has partially succeeded, to apply an exacting, mathematical standard to a process that is not conducive to it. In addition, it wrongly gave a perception that there was a single standard to use when grading coins, when in fact there was not. Still, the coin market continues to have basic guidelines that have been incorporated into industry standards that individual buyers, sellers and grading services use when they evaluate a rare coin.

Dr. Sheldon devised a scale based on the numbers 1 through 70, which he intended to roughly correlate with some of the adjectival descriptions. However, unlike the adjectives, which had no reference to price, Dr. Sheldon's methodology was specifically designed to refer to prices. For example, a coin in fine-12 condition is designed to be equivalent to one-fifth the price of an uncirculated-60 coin, even if the wear on the coin is nowhere near as substantial as the numbers might suggest.

In any event, the numbers took on an abbreviated short-hand that is still widely used in the marketplace. It is important to know that the meaning of the numbers has changed, and is subject to different interpreations.

For an approximation of grading numbers, with their adjectival equivalents, as utilized in the revised version of the *Sheldon Grading Guide,* imagine a one foot long ruler. The grade poor-1 is at the zero inch mark, and uncirculated 60 is at the 11 inch point. (The remaining grades of uncirculated are on each smaller scale line from 11 through 12 inches only).

The ranges are:

- uncirculated, 60, 65, and 70;
- about uncirculated, 50 to 55;
- extremely fine, 40 to 45;
- very fine, 20 to 30;
- fine, 12 to 15;
- very good, 7 to 10;
- good, 4 to 6;
- very fair, 3 to 5;
- fair-2; and
- poor-1.

Below is what this would look like linearly:

Poor	Good	Fine	Very Fine	XF	AU	MS	MS	MS	MS
1	6	12	30	40	55	60	63	65	70

In time, modifications were made to the Sheldon scale in order to describe and grade a coin that was in a slightly better state of preservation than another. For example, though originally not officially sanctioned by any organization, AU-58 and AU-59 are about uncirculated coins whose appearance is substantially better than an about uncirculated-55 coin, but appear to have sufficient surface wear for the coin not to be classified as uncirculated, or MS-60. For that reason, the American Numismatic Association (the largest educational non-profit organization of coin collectors in the world) added that grade to its repertoire by motion of its board of directors. It is a grade widely utilized in the marketplace. The same rationale was used to introduce MS-61, and MS-62, two grades of uncirculated that are better than "just" uncirculated, but not yet choice.

In the marketplace several modifications of the Sheldon standard also have taken place. For example, in the mid-1970s, the "Kosoff Commentary" column in *Coin World* frequently assaulted the then-pervasive practice in newspaper advertising of calling coins MS-70. (The MS-70 coin is literally perfect). Then, as now, there was no definitive reference point—no fixed statute or standard for the seller, or the buyer to refer to. There were only guideposts, of which the Sheldon guide, and its imitators were a few.

The first of the major written interpretations of the Sheldon system of numbering (for Kosoff and other dealers utilized their own personal modifications for more than twenty-five years without even trying to codify them) was the *ANA Grading Guide*. This book looked at all series of U.S. coins and then went on to divide uncirculated coins into three major categories:

- MS-70 (perfect uncirculated). MS-70, a perfect uncirculated, is the finest quality available. Such a coin under 4X magnification will show no bag marks or lines or other evidence of handling or contact with other coins.

- MS-65 (choice uncirculated). This refers to an above average uncirculated coin, which may be brilliant or toned (and described accordingly) and which has fewer bag marks than usual; scattered occasional bag marks on the surface or perhaps one or two very light rim marks may be visible.

- MS-60 (uncirculated). MS-60 or uncirculated (typical uncirculated without any other adjectives) refers to a coin that has a moderate number of bag marks on its surface. Also present may be a few minor edge nicks and marks, though not of a serious nature. Unusually deep bag marks, nicks and the like must be separately described. The coin may be either brilliant or toned.

By the time that the second edition was published in 1981, it was clear that there had been a change in grading interpretations. The result was that the Sheldon system was varied still further. A new classification, MS-67, called "gem uncirculated" was added, and is used when describing "a coin which is midway between MS-70 and MS-65. The coin may be either brilliant or toned . . ."

One major periodical, *COINage* magazine, believes that it is essential for its readers (and prospective buyers from the advertising) to understand what it is that they are purchasing, and what the descriptions of the coins actually consist of. Consistent with this philosophy, *COINage* has set forth standards that require its advertisers to disclose what the grading numbers mean and what standards are employed during the grading process. At the front of its September, 1997 issue, for example, *COINage* provides a "notice to coin buyers" that explains the different types of standards that are used within the periodical. Specifically, the notice proclaims:

> Uncirculated coins have no visible signs of wear, though they may have blemishes, bag marks, rim nicks, tarnish or even be weakly struck (which often resembles wear). In uncirculated condition, there are many different grading opinions, some of which are described adjectivally, others with numbers. Not all grades have the identical meaning. This depends on the grading standard utilized.

Emphasising the fact that grading and pricing are not at all synonymous, the notice states further: "The value of the item to the buyer should be determined by the price, not the grade."

Current Grading Methods Used in *COINage* Magazine

In examining the *COINage* magazine grading guide, which is typical of various other periodicals, there are currently five different grading services or standards that are specifically mentioned, some of which are registered trademarks or used under license. These include:

- *American Numismatic Association Grading Guide,*
- Amos Numismatic Authentication and Certification Service,
- *Photograde* by James F. Ruddy,
- Numismatic Certification Institute (NCI),
- Numismatic Guaranty Corporation (NGC), and
- Professional Coin Grading Service, or PCGS.

The magazine, however, warns that "if there is no symbol or other explanation, the reader must assume that the advertisers grading standards are based upon their own personal experience."

It is undeniable that the grading of coins is important to buyers, sellers, dealers, collectors and investors alike, and certainly is important as you make purchases for your rare coin retirement portfolio. Yet the process of grading is little more than a bazaar in which the buyer and the seller are each entitled to have their own opinion, and each can accept or reject the other's analysis of grade and price.

Changes over Time

That grading has changed over time is clearly illustrated by an example taken from an auction sale conducted by the legendary A. Kosoff. The year was 1963, and an auction was held by the Numismatic Association of Southern California. The Lahrman Collection was being sold by Kosoff, and it included a 1793 large cent (Sheldon variety 11-A): quite a scarce piece. Earlier, the piece was in the Oscar J. Pearl Collection sold by Numismatic Gallery. (Abe Kosoff was a partner in Numismatic Gallery with Abner Kreisberg). When the coin was sold in the Pearl Collection, it was catalogued F-12 (meaning fine-12). Utilizing the same Sheldon numbering standards in 1963, cataloger Abe Kosoff, after first noting its grade in the Pearl sale, stated, "it is fine-15."

The problem with numerical grading, of course, is that it gives the impression of exactitude and precision when it is, in the final analysis, little more than a subjective view of the cataloger. As I stated in a column in *Numismatic News* in 1975: "Standards, no matter how precisely defined, nonetheless remain subjective. Differences of opinion, not only between collectors and dealers, but even between dealers themselves, are bound to arise."

Unlike many other objets d'art, the condition or state of preservation of a coin cannot be improved. Metal cannot be added to or "repaired" without the coin losing a substantial part of its collecting value. Unlike paintings or sculpture, which can be repaired in a virtually undetectable manner, and where the effect on value is minimal, a repaired or "improved" coin—or one that is shined with metal polish—loses much of its value.

In planning your rare coin retirement, try to pick the best condition you can afford within your budget. Poor condition is the least impressive state of preservation, and can commonly be referred to as a worn coin, like the buffalo nickels—dateless with little facial or other detail—that frequently appeared in pocket change three decades ago.

Uncirculated is the best condition, though it is not fully descriptive of what the term actually means. Technically, the coin cannot be said to be "without any circulation," since it is the act of placing the coin in circulation that removes it from the mint. Rather, uncirculated refers to an absence of wear on the metal surface of the coin, means that the coin has not been in general circulation.

Debate about Degrees of Uncirculated

Precisely how a coin is graded or described is the subject of considerable debate, though there is less debate over whether a coin is "uncirculated" or "circulated" than over the degrees within those various categories. What, though, about the uncirculated grade and coins like silver dollars, or other coins that are to be included in your rare coin retirement portfolio? The commentators differ on how to describe differing types of uncirculated coins.

Dr. Richard Doty refers to "MS-65s, sometimes called 'choice un-circulateds,' . . . [which] will command much higher prices than MS-60s. . . ." (p. 151). In *Rare Coin Investment Strategy* (1986), Scott Travers terms "Choice Mint State-65" the "most frequently traded investor-quality coin," using the same standards that are employed by the American Numismatic Association's grading standards, but then goes on to state that,

> Although A.N.A. grading standards indicate that an MS-65 may be lightly finger marked, the marketplace often dictates that MS-65 be virtually mark-free. . . . Although A.N.A. standards indicate otherwise, an MS-65 is generally expected to exhibit all of the detail that the mint intended it to display . . .

In Mort Reed's book, *Coins: An Investors & Collector's Guide* (1973), James F. Ruddy was invited to contribute a chapter on coin grading and noted that,

> Certain early coins are extremely difficult to find in Uncirculated condition without any bag marks or handling. Such flawless pieces are sometimes designated as Choice Uncirculated or Gem Uncirculated. Choice describes an above average Uncirculated specimen, well struck and with a minimum of minor bag marks or minting defects. Gem Uncirculated is the finest available, a sharply struck coin that is free of the usual minor bag marks or minting defects.

In *A Penny Whimsy,* Dr. Sheldon (who, after all, invented the numerical grading scale) said something quite different:

> The MS-65 is a coin that would be a perfect MS-70 except for some small minor blemish. It may lack full mint luster, or some microscopic or almost negligible blemish may be demonstrable. There may be a spot of discoloration, a fingermark or a barely discernable nick.

A later writer, James Halperin, in *N.C.I. Grading Guide* (1986) notes that "choice" uncirculated is used by the ANA to denote coins that are MS-65 or proof-65, however he also notes that

"Many dealers apply the terms to MS/proof-63 and call MS/proof-65 coins 'gem.'" Thus, if the numbers mean differing states of preservation (even when consistently used), the adjectives are not precise and may have different meanings. Jeffrey J. Pritchard in *Heads You Win, Tails You Win: The Inside Secrets of Rare Coin Investing* (1983) simply sums up prevailing opinion when he states that grading of uncirculated coins "remains somewhat arbitrary, even among so-called experts."

The widely respected author, Q. David Bowers, who served as president of both the Professional Numismatists Guild, and the American Numismatic Association, writes in *Adventures with Rare Coins 259*, (1979),

> Often five different sellers will assign five different grades to the same coin, perhaps differing just slightly but still differing, often with important financial consequences . . . As the evaluation of the grade or condition of a coin is a largely subjective matter, experts can legitimately differ . . .

Eleven Gradations of Uncirculated

The third edition of *Official A.N.A. Standards for United States Coins* (1987) made a number of substantive changes to its grading system. In particular, it adopted an eleven point system for uncirculated United States coins using a scale of 60 to 70. The guide notes that uncirculated coins are generally graded in accordance with five major categories (same previously utilized, MS-60, MS-63, MS-65, MS-67, and MS-70), but that as of June, 1986, some (but not all) U.S. coins could be graded on an eleven point scale. The book notes that these include Morgan and Peace silver dollars, Liberty and Saint-Gaudens Double Eagles or $20 gold pieces, and Morgan Liberty half dollars. By 1997, not only had eleven uncirculated grades spread to all series, but there had been attempts at computerized grading that involved determining condition down to nearly tenth of a grade (i.e., MS-64.2, MS-64.4, and so on).

What Goes into a Grading Decision

Virtually all standards consider strike, color, toning, and value, but these "are considered to be too subjective for consistent evaluation under the *Official A.N.A. Standards*." The ANA standards for uncirculated coins are as follows:

- **MS-60**   Unattractive, dull or washed-out mint luster may mark this coin. There may be many ugly or large contact marks, or damage spots, but absolutely no trace of wear. There could be heavy concentrations of hairlines, or unattractive large areas of scuff marks. Rim nicks may be present, and eye appeal is very poor. Copper coins may be dark, dull and spotted.

- **MS-61**   Mint luster may be diminished or noticeably impaired, and the surface has clusters of large and small contact marks throughout. Hairlines could be very noticeable. Scuff marks may show as unattractive patches on large areas or major features. Small rim nicks may show, and the quality may be noticeably poor. Eye appeal is quite unattractive. Copper pieces will be generally dark and possibly spotted.

- **MS-62**   An impaired or dull luster may be evident. Clusters of small marks are seen throughout with a few large marks or nicks in prime focal areas. Hairlines may be very noticeable. Large unattractive scuff marks might be seen on major features, and the quality may be noticeably below average. Overall eye appeal is generally acceptable. Copper coins will show a diminished color and tone.

- **MS-63**   Starts Choice Uncircluated Grade. Mint luster may be slightly impaired. Numerous small contact marks, and a few scattered heavy marks may be seen. Small hairlines are visible without magnification. Several detracting scuff marks may be present throughout the design or in the fields. The general quality is slightly below average, but overall the coin is rather attractive. Copper pieces will retain parts of the original color.

- MS-64   Full average luster for the type is necessary. Several small contact marks in groups, as well as one or two heavy marks may be present. One or two small patches of hairlines may show under low magnification. Noticeable scuff marks might be seen throughout the design or in the field. Average overall quality with a pleasing eye appeal. Copper coins may be slightly dull but show original color.

- MS-65   Starts "Gem" grade. Shows attractive average quality of luster for the type. A few small scattered contact marks or two larger marks may be present, and one or two small patches of hairlines may show under magnification. Noticeable scuff marks may show on the high points of the design. Overall quality is above average and overall eye appeal is very pleasing. Copper coins must have full original color and tone.

- MS-66   Must have above average quality full original mint luster, with no more than two or three noticeable contact marks. A few very light hairlines may show under magnification. There may be one or two light scuff marks showing on frosted surfaces or in the field. The eye appeal must be above average for the date and mint. Copper coins display full original color and tone.

- MS-67   Has full original luster for date and mint. May have three or four very small contact marks and one more noticeable but not detracting mark. On comparable coins, one or two small single hairlines may show under magnification or one or two partially hidden scuff marks may be present. Eye appeal is exceptional. Copper coins have lustrous original color.

- MS-68   Attractive full original luster for date and mint, with no more than four light scattered contact marks. No hairlines or scuff marks show. Exceptional eye appeal. Copper coins must have lustrous original color.

- MS-69   Must have very attractive full original luster for the date and mint, with no more than two small non-detracting contact marks. Absolutely no hairlines or scuff marks can be seen. Attractive with exceptional eye ap-

peal. Copper coins must be bright with full original color
and blazing luster.

- MS-70   The perfect coin. Has very attractive full original
luster of the highest quality for the date and mint. No
contact marks are visible under magnification. There are
absolutely no hairlines or scuff marks. Attractive and outstanding eye appeal. Copper coins must be bright with
full original color and blazing luster.

Explanation of Components to Grading

In addition to this description of the ANA standards a chart
is provided in the third edition showing matters such as luster, eye
appeal, hairlines, and contact or bag marks in order to attempt a
modest comparison with some other standards,

- Eye appeal runs from poor to outstanding, with mid-
points showing the eye appeal becoming rather attractive
at MS-63, very pleasing at MS-65, and exceptional at MS-
67 (formerly "gem"), and above. At MS-70, it is obviously
outstanding.

- Luster on the coin may (in MS-60) be either original or
impaired, but must be fully original starting at MS-64.
After that, luster rises from above average to attractive, to
a superior state.

- "Hairlines," visible typically under magnification, are taken
into account and, as a result, an MS-60 coin may have "noticeable patch or continuous hair lining throughout," which
is acceptable up to the ANA standards of MS-65. Above the
level of what was formerly referred to as "choice," no hairlines are visible without magnification.

An MS-60 coin is expected to have heavy surface marking.
At choice (MS-65 on the ANA scale) light or scattered contact
marks are permissible. At the gem level, three or four miniscule
contact marks are permissible or one or two in a prime focal area.
At MS-70, none show under magnification.

The New Numeric Scale

It is interesting to note that, quite apart from the comments made previously, as of the third edition of the *Official ANA Standards,* "the ANA standard numerical scale is divided into the following steps: 3, 4, 8, 12, 20, 30, 40, 45, 50, 55, 58, 60, 61, 62, 63, 64, 65, 66, 67, 68, 69 and 70." Intermediate grades for the circulated pieces are still "not recognized" on the basis that "grading is not that precise, and using such finely split intermediate grades is imparting a degree of accuracy that will probably not be able to be verified by the numismatists," and is entirely consistent with the views expressed in prior editions.

It is equally interesting to note, however, that despite the use of each of these numbers, the guide still states that "for most coins such minor divisions as MS-61, MS-62 and so on cannot be adhered to with consistency," but goes on to note, "however, the official ANA Grading System does recognize all numbers from MS-60 through MS-70 may be used." It further clarifies this by stating that "even the most advanced numismatists cannot consistently agree on such narrow classifications as MS-61, MS-62, MS-68 or MS-69, and for this reason, minute distinctions of this nature are not incorporated in the general text. These distinctions are simply too exacting to permit accurate descriptions at this time."

Different Strokes

How is it that coin grade descriptions, and hence opinions, can differ?

Grading a coin is inherently subjective and represents one person's view as to its state of preservation, and, if uncirculated, the degree or extent of pleasure (eye appeal) that it brings to the examiner. Ultimately, this is translated into a price at which the grader would purchase, or sell the coin. Yet, grade is not dependent on price, and price is not dependent on grade. Rather, it is a classic economic transaction, truly dependent upon the sum of the parts suggested by the seller and agreed to by the buyer.

Today, the situation is not that different than it was in 1913, when H.O. Granberg wrote to propose a uniform standard for classifying the condition of coins. In sum, the grade of a coin, then, as now, is an opinion, which can and does vary from expert to expert.

In planning your rare coin retirement portfolio, opting for the best grade that you can afford is usually a good bet, but it is important to recall that you need to learn about grading to assure yourself that what you have bought represents a good value. If you do not, you will have to rely on third party grading and certification services for their opinion as to the grade. In any case, it is important to recall that on February 19, 1986, the ANA Board, by resolution, approved the following statement:

> Grading is an art and not an exact science. More precisely, grading is a matter of opinion. Differences of opinion may occur among graders as to a particular coin, and any grader could conceivably change his interpretation of the grading standards over the years.
>
> When the *ANA Official Grading Standards for United States Coins* book was published in 1978, it represented a new grading system, previously untried.
>
> The grading standards as enumerated in the book were and are not precise, with the descriptions lending themselves to different interpretations. The marketplace composed of collectors and dealers has tightened its interpretation in recent years and ANACS [the ANA Certification Service] has reflected those changes. Accordingly, the ANA Grading Service, endeavoring to keep in step with current market interpretations (rather than create interpretations of its own) has in recent times graded coins more conservatively than in the past, in many instances.
>
> Hence, it may be the situation that a coin which was graded MS-65 by the Grading Service in 1981 or 1982, for example, may, if regraded in 1985 or 1986, merit the current interpretation of MS-63 or less. Similarly, dealers and others in the commercial sector have found that coins that they graded MS-65 several years ago may merit MS-63 or lower interpretations today.

It is important to remember, however, that a third party certification and grade is not a panacea. A coin graded MS-65 by ANACS is not necessarily the same price as a coin graded by PCGS (the

Professional Coin Grading Service), and a PCGS-graded coin may not be the same price as one graded by the Numismatic Certification Institute (NCI) or Numismatic Guaranty Corporation (NGC). NCI utilizes standards that differ from those contained in the ANA grading guide, but which are set forth in its own grading book. PCGS utilizes unpublished standards that differ from those found in the ANA grading guide or the NCI grading guide. NGC utilizes unpublished standards that differ from each of the foregoing. There are other grading services as well, whose grading and pricing differs from these other, better-known services.

Grading Changes of the 1980s

By the start of the 1980s a number of market innovations were made to the Sheldon numerical system, and the adjectival version that worked side-by-side with it. The ANA reflected these realities in the revised edition of its *Grading Guide.* A new MS-65 was referred to as choice uncirculated and was described as "an above average uncirculated coin which may be brilliant or toned (and described accordingly) and which has fewer bag marks than usual; scattered occasional bag marks on the surface or perhaps one or two very light rim marks."

An MS-63, or "select uncirculated" was added and used to describe a coin between MS-65 and MS-60, followed again by the MS-60 typical uncirculated piece.

Size Counts Too

Different coin designs are also graded differently, though the general principals that are applied are identical. Collectors of nineteenth century type coins know that if the word "Liberty" on the coin is fully readable, the coin is typically in "fine" condition. When only three letters in Liberty, are distinct, the coin is described as "very good." This is true whether the coin is an Indian Head cent, a half dime, or a large sized half dollar. This holds true for gold pieces, and indeed, all coins where the motto "Liberty" is emblazoned within the design, rather than in the field. Each coin design, denomination, and type, wears differently. It is natural to expect that a 25-cent piece, used as pocket change, has a larger surface that is more prone to damage than a half dime, which is of a wholly different size: the dime has a diameter of a 15.5 mm., compared to 24.3 mm. for the quarter. Similarly, a silver 3-cent piece, with a 14 mm. diameter, has a lot less surface space than a half dollar minted in the middle of the nineteenth century, with a 30.6 mm. diameter. Although the diameters are just about half, or double, depending upon your perspective, the surface area (when expressed in square millimeters) shows the dramatic difference: 153.86 sq. mm. for the 3-cent piece, or trime, and 735 sq. mm. for the half dollar.

The following letter, written by a serious numismatist, says it all:

> It is very important to the members of the A.N.A. that the Board of Governors take some stand with reference to issuing some kind of statement classifying coins so that all dealers that catalogue and sell coins at auction must use the same classification.
> *Letter to the editor by C. E. Bunnell, 26 The Numismatist 81*
> *(1913).*

In essence, the problem as described nearly ninety years ago continues, and it is unlikely that in the future there will be a unified standard within the field.

Where to Purchase
Coins for your
Rare Coin Retirement

You've probably decided that you want to do more than *plan* your rare coin retirement: you want to start making the purchases that will allow it to *happen*. But where do you begin?

Assuming that you are satisfied with your ability to either grade coins yourself, or you plan to purchase only those coins that have been graded and authenticated by a third-party grading service, your next step is to locate a coin dealer.

You could look in the Yellow Pages of a telephone book, or even get a word-of-mouth recommendation, but if you prefer to find someone whose reputation has been reviewed first, there are some other approaches that you can take.

If you have access to the internet, the American Numismatic Association has a list of dealer-members that can be accessed based on specialty or location. The address of the ANA on the world wide web is: http://www.money.org The ANA also has a toll-free telephone number that you can use to get comparable information: 800-367-9723.

Should you desire information directly from a dealer organization, the not-for-profit Professional Numismatists Guild, Inc., can be of assistance. Their address and telephone number is:

Professional Numismatists Guild, Inc.
3950 Concordia Lane
Fallbrook, CA 92028:
Fax (619) 728-8507
Tel (619) 728-1300
http://web.coin-universe.com/png

The Industry Council for Tangible Assets (ICTA), a watch-dog and lobbying organization also maintains a list of supporting members. There are many other dealers and organizations. In the interest of disclosure, I served as the American Numismatic Association's legislative counsel.

A Chart of Possibilities
for Your Rare Coin Portfolio

As you start to think about planning your rare coin retirement, there is a lot to consider. Do you include gold and platinum coinage in your rare coin retirement? Do you go with gold to the exclusion of all else? What is your focus?

The master chart that follows lists the coins that are included in this book, or are otherwise mentioned. There's a special list of 100 gold and platinum coins assembled at a total cost of about $10,000, which could well be your golden rare coin retirement. But there are many other coins that also could be satisfactorily added to your rare coin portfolio. That choice is yours.

The coins that follow have an average cost of $100 or less—so you can pick and choose according to your budget, and your predilection. By varying condition, you can get a slightly different mix too.

Except for the foreign gold coins, which are not given individual coverage in this book, nearly all of the other coins are given extensive treatment in the main text of the book. Some contemporary commemorative coins are treated in a single chapter on low mintage modern issues; some of the others are given more extensive treatment. Other older commemoratives are also discussed in a single chapter for your convenience.

The Chart

Date	Mintmark	Type	Denomination	Condition	Quantity	Cost Each	Total
1923	P	Peace	$1	MS65	1	$130	$130
1922	P	Peace	$1	MS64	2	$40	$80
1922	D	Peace	$1	MS64	1	$70	$70
1923	P	Peace	$1	MS64	2	$40	$80
1926	S	Peace	$1	MS63	1	$57	$57
1935	P	Peace	$1	MS63	1	$68	$68
1902	P	Barber	10¢	MS63	1	$100	$100
1903	P	Barber	10¢	MS63	1	$100	$100
1904	P	Barber	10¢	MS63	1	$100	$100
1905	P	Barber	10¢	MS63	1	$100	$100
1906	P	Barber	10¢	MS63	1	$100	$100
1907	P	Barber	10¢	MS63	1	$100	$100
1908	P	Barber	10¢	MS63	1	$100	$100
1909	P	Barber	10¢	MS63	1	$100	$100
1910	P	Barber	10¢	MS63	1	$100	$100
1911	P	Barber	10¢	MS63	1	$100	$100
1912	P	Barber	10¢	MS63	1	$100	$100
1913	P	Barber	10¢	MS63	1	$100	$100
1914	P	Barber	10¢	MS63	1	$100	$100
1915	P	Barber	10¢	MS63	1	$100	$100
1916	P	Barber	10¢	MS63	1	$100	$100
1908	D	Barber	10¢	MS63	1	$120	$120
1911	D	Barber	10¢	MS63	1	$120	$120
1912	D	Barber	10¢	MS63	1	$120	$120
1911	S	Barber	10¢	MS63	1	$105	$105
1916	S	Barber	10¢	MS63	1	$105	$105
1991		1/4 oz	($10)	MS63	1	$99	$99
1970	D	Kennedy	50¢	MS63	9	$11	$99
1970	S	Kennedy	50¢	MS63	9	$8	$72
1964 to 1996		Kennedy 50¢ Set (100 coins)		BU	1	$300	$300
1989	D	Congressional	50¢	BU	8	$12	$96
1993		Madison Lettered Edge	50¢	BU	1	$300	$300
		Foreign Gold Coins (various)		Varies	1	$85	$85
1994	P	Vietnam Memorial	50¢	BU	3	$27	$81
1993		1994 Jefferson 250th	$1	BU	3	$31	$93
1995		Double Die Cent	1¢	MS65	4	$25	$100
1972		Double Die Cent	1¢	AU50	1	$145	$145
1881	S	Morgan	$1	MS63	3	$28	$84
1878	CC	Morgan	$1	MS63	1	$82	$82
1879	CC	Morgan	$1	VF	1	$100	$100
1880	CC	Morgan	$1	MS60	1	$130	$130
1881	CC	Morgan	$1	MS60	1	$143	$143
1882	CC	Morgan	$1	MS64	1	$76	$76

Date	Mintmark	Type	Denomination	Condition	Quantity	Cost Each	Total
1883	CC	Morgan	$1	MS64	1	$76	$76
1884	CC	Morgan	$1	MS64	1	$76	$76
1885	CC	Morgan	$1	AU50	1	$155	$155
1965 to date		Washington 25¢ Set		BU & Pf	1	$155	$155
1941-'64		Washington 25¢ Set		BU	1	$260	$260
1979-'81		S.B. Anthony Set	$1	BU	1	$135	$135
1981	P	S.B. Anthony	$1	BU	20	$3	$55
1981	D	S.B. Anthony	$1	BU	20	$3	$55
1981	S	S.B. Anthony	$1	BU	20	$3	$55
1971-'78		Ike dollar set	$1	BU & Pf	1	$105	$105
1938-'65		Jeff. Nickel set	5¢	BU	1	$130	$130
1934-'58		Lincoln cent set	1¢	BU	1	$60	$60
1959-'97		Lincoln cent set	1¢	BU & Pf	1	$120	$120
1904	O	Morgan	$1	MS65	1	$95	$95
1904	P	Indian cent	1¢	MS65	1	$50	$50
1904	P	Indian cent	1¢	Pf-64	1	$95	$95
1946-'65		FDR Dime Set		BU	1	$100	$100
1901	P	Indian cent	1¢	MS65	1	$50	$50
1902	P	Indian cent	1¢	MS65	1	$50	$50
1903	P	Indian cent	1¢	MS65	1	$50	$50
1905	P	Indian cent	1¢	MS65	1	$50	$50
1906	P	Indian cent	1¢	MS65	1	$50	$50
1907	P	Indian cent	1¢	MS65	1	$50	$50
1908	P	Indian cent	1¢	MS65	1	$50	$50
1909	P	Indian cent	1¢	MS65	1	$50	$50
1900	P	Indian cent	1¢	Pf-64	1	$95	$95
1901	P	Indian cent	1¢	Pf-64	1	$95	$95
1902	P	Indian cent	1¢	Pf-64	1	$95	$95
1903	P	Indian cent	1¢	Pf-64	1	$95	$95
1905	P	Indian cent	1¢	Pf-64	1	$95	$95
1906	P	Indian cent	1¢	Pf-64	1	$95	$95
1907	P	Indian cent	1¢	Pf-64	1	$95	$95
1908	P	Indian cent	1¢	Pf-64	1	$95	$95
1994		Turks & Caicos	Platinum		1	$50	$50
1986-'96		Silver eagles (Gem proof)-12 coins		Pf-65	12	$300	$3,600
1989		Isle of Man	1/25 crown	BU	1	$22	$22
1996		Isle of Man	1/25 crown	BU	1	$22	$22
1896	Australia	Sovereign		Unc.	1	$110	$110
1881A	Austria	8 Florin/20 Francs		XF	1	$87	$87
	Austria	1 Ducat		XF-AU	1	$44	$44
1915	Austria	1 Ducat (restrike)		BU	1	$43	$43
1974	Bahamas		$100	Proof	1	$130	$130
1975	Barbados		$100	Proof	1	$60	$60

Date	Mintmark	Type	Denomination	Condition	Quantity	Cost Each	Total
	Belgium	20 Francs		XF-AU	1	$70	$70
1981	Belize	national Independence	$100	Proof	1	$125	$125
1981	Belize		$100	Proof	1	$40	$40
1985	Belize		$100	Proof	1	$45	$45
1975	Bermuda		$100	Proof	1	$105	$105
1977	Bermuda		$50	Proof	1	$75	$75
1952	Bolivia	7 Gramos		BU	1	$95	$95
1981	Brit. Virgin Islands		$50	Proof	1	$55	$55
1975	Brit. Virgin Islands		$100	Proof	1	$100	$100
1894	Bulgaria	10 Leva		VF	1	$100	$100
	Canada	1/15 oz. Maple Leaf		BU or Pf	1	$58	$58
	Canada	1/10 oz. Platinum Maple Leaf		BU	1	$53	$53
1987	Canada	Olympic	$100	Proof	1	$99	$99
	Canada	1/10 oz Platinum Lynx	$30	Proof	1	$110	$110
1989	Canada	Indian			1	$94	$94
1976	Canada	Olympic	$100	Unc.	1	$97	$97
	Cayman Islands		$25	BU	1	$83	$83
1913	Columbia		5 Pesos	AU	1	$105	$105
1976	Comoros		10,000 Francs	Proof	1	$125	$125
1975	Cook Islands		$100	Proof	1	$130	$130
1988	Cook Islands	Bison		Proof	1	$45	$45
1916	Cuba		2 Pesos	BU	1	$119	$119
1930	Egypt		100 Piastres	AU	1	$100	$100
1971	El Salvador	50 Colonies		Proof	1	$100	$100
1971	El Salvador	25 Colonies		Proof	1	$75	$75
1970	Equatorial Guinea		250 Pesetas	Proof	1	$100	$100
1882	Finland	100 Maarka		BU	1	$99	$99
1801	France	(AN 12A)	12 Francs	VF	1	$125	$125
1815	France	Bordeaux Louis XVIII	20 Francs	VF	1	$115	$115
1814	France		20 Francs	XF	1	$95	$95
1886	France	(3d Republic)	20 Francs	AU	1	$78	$78
	France		20 Francs	XF-AU	1	$70	$709
1899-1914	France	Rooster	20 Francs	BU	1	$80	$80
1856	France		5 Francs	VF	1	$51	$51
	Germany		10 Marks	BU	1	$115	$115
	Germany		20 Marks	XF-AU	1	$85	$85
1997	Gibralter	Classical heads (set of 4)			1	$198	$198
	Great Britain	Sovereign Eliz II		XF-AU	1	$84	$84
	Great Britain	Sovereign Old Style		XF-AU	1	$87	$87
1989	Great Britain	Sovereign		Proof	1	$100	$100

Date	Mintmark	Type	Denomination	Condition	Quantity	Cost Each	Total
1986	Great Britain	1/2 Sovereign		Proof	1	$61	$61
1981	Guernsey		£1	Proof	1	$125	$125
1970	Guinea		1000 Francs	Proof	1	$75	$75
1976	Guyana		$100	Proof	1	$50	$50
1973	Haiti	200 Gourdes		Proof	1	$75	$75
1973	Haiti	100 Gourdes		Proof	1	$60	$60
1885	Hungary		20 Fr/8 Florin	XF	1	$82	$82
1918	India	Sovereign		BU	1	$105	$105
1322	Iran		5000 Dinars	XF	1	$75	$75
1342	Iran	AH	1/2 Toman	VF-XF	1	$39	$39
1971	Iran		500 Rials (Fr 109)	Proof	1	$125	$125
	Italy		20 Lire	XF-AU	1	$68	$68
1975	Jamaica		$100	Proof	1	$100	$100
1835	Japan		2 Shu	XF	1	$52	$52
1977	Liberia		$100	Proof	1	$125	$125
1953	Luxembourg	(KM #1M)	20 Francs	BU	1	$100	$100
1976	Malaysia		200 Ringgit	Proof	1	$100	$100
1974	Malta		20 Pounds	Proof	1	$90	$90
1974	Malta		10 Pounds	Proof	1	$60	$60
	Mexico		2 Pesos	BU	1	$25	$25
1906	Mexico		5 Pesos	Unc.	1	$55	$55
1946	Mexico		2 1/2 Pesos	BU	1	$42	$42
1905	Mexico		10 Pesos	XF-AU	1	$99	$99
	Mexico		5 Pesos	BU	1	$43	$43
	Mexico		10 Pesos	BU	1	$83	$83
	Mexico		2 1/2 Pesos	BU	1	$33	$33
1985	Mexico		250 Pesos	BU	1	$99	$99
	Netherlands		10 Guilder	XF-AU	1	$73	$73
1988	Netherlands		2 Ducats	Proof	1	$120	$120
1975	Netherlands		1 Ducat	Proof	1	$60	$60
1979	Netherlands Antilles		50 Gulden	BU	1	$40	$40
1975	Panama		100 Balboas	Proof	1	$90	$90
1975	Papua New Guinea		100 Kina	Proof	1	$110	$110
1965	Peru		100 Soles	BU	1	$65	$65
	Russia	Nicholas II	5 Rubles	XF-AU	1	$48	$48
1964	S. Africa	Proof Set		Proof	1	$135	$135
1961-'83	South Africa	1/4 oz.	2 Rands	BU	1	$88	$88
1894	South Africa	1/2 Pound		VF	1	$75	$75
1982	South Africa	Krugerrand 1/10 oz.		BU	1	$43	$43
1878	Spain	Alfonso XII (Fr 343R)		BU	1	$85	$85
1978	Sudan	(Fr 4)	25 Pounds	Proof	1	$135	$135
	Switzerland		20 Francs	XF-AU	1	$70	$70
	Switzerland		10 Francs	XF-AU	1	$100	$100
1969	Turkey		50 Kurish	MS64	1	$75	$75

Date	Mintmark	Type	Denomination	Condition	Quantity	Cost Each	Total
1976	Turks & Caicos	50 Crowns		Proof	1	$100	$100
1981	Turks & Caicos	100 Crowns		Proof	1	$90	$90
1976	Turks & Caicos	25 Crowns		Proof	1	$75	$75
1987	USA	Constitution commemorative $5		BU or Pf	1	$99	$99
1997	USA	Gold 1/10 oz Eagle		BU	1	$43	$43
1997	USA	Gold 1/4 oz Eagle		BU	1	$96	$96
1849-'54	USA	Type 1	$1	VF	1	$103	$103
1908-'29	USA	1/2 Indian	$2	VF	1	$119	$119
1905	Venezuela	(Fr 6)	20 Bolivares	MS64	1	$100	$100
1789	Venice	Zecchino (Fr. 1445)		VF-XF	1	$155	$155
1982	Yugoslavia		5000 Dinara	Proof	1	$100	$100
1899	U.S.	Liberty	$5	MS60	1	$144	$144
1900	U.S.	Liberty	$5	MS60	1	$144	$144
1901	U.S.S	Liberty	$5	MS60	1	$144	$144
1902	U.S.S	Liberty	$5	MS60	1	$144	$144
1903	U.S.	Liberty	$5	MS60	1	$144	$144
1903	U.S.S	Liberty	$5	MS60	1	$144	$144
1904	U.S.	Liberty	$5	MS60	1	$144	$144
1906	U.S.	Liberty	$5	MS60	1	$144	$144
1906	U.S.D	Liberty	$5	MS60	1	$144	$144
1907	U.S.	Liberty	$5	MS60	1	$144	$144
1907	U.S.D	Liberty	$5	MS60	1	$144	$144
1908		Liberty	$5	MS60	1	$144	$144
1996	Community Service		$1	BU	1	$144	$144
1993	Madison		$5	BU	1	$144	$144
1994	World War II		$5	BU	1	$144	$144
1995	Olympic	(track)	$1	BU	1	$35	$35
1992	Columbus		$5	BU	1	$144	$144
1992	Olympic		$5	BU	1	$144	$144
1995	Olympic-Blind Runner		$1	BU	1	$35	$35
1996	Smithsonian		$1	BU	1	$35	$35
1991	Mt Rushmore		$5	BU	1	$144	$144
1995	Olympic-Gymnastics		$1	BU	1	$35	$35
1989	Congressionial		$5	BU	1	$35	$35
1996	Olympic-Swimming		$1	BU	1	$35	$35
1996	Olympic-Soccer		$1	BU	1	$35	$35
1995	Civil War Battles		$1	BU	1	$35	$35

Date	Mintmark	Type	Denomination	Condition	Quantity	Cost Each	Total
1994	Women in Military		$1	BU	1	$35	$35
1994	POW		$1	BU	1	$35	$35
1994	Vietnam		$1	BU	1	$35	$35
1988	Olympic		$5	BU	1	$144	$144
1994	Capitol Bicentennial		$1	BU	1	$35	$35
1994	World Cup		$1	BU	1	$35	$35
1995	Special Olympics		$1	BU	1	$35	$35
1994	World War II		$1	BU	1	$35	$35
1986	Statue of Liberty		$5	BU	1	$35	$35
1993	Madison		$1	BU	1	$35	$35
			Average Price			$96	
			Total portfolio cost				$21,712

Carson City Silver Dollars

1878-CC (MS-63, $82)
1879-CC (VF, $100)
1880-CC (MS-60, $130)
1881-CC (MS-60, $143)
1882-CC (MS-64, $76)
1883-CC (MS-64, $76)
1884-CC (MS-64 $76)
1885-CC (AU-50, $155)

For an average price of $104 a coin, you can acquire eight coins with a long history and good potential for profitability: a short set of eight Carson City Mint silver dollars. These are the coins that Jesse James and his gang sought to rob from local banks, and that Wyatt Earp may have used while playing poker in old Tombstone, Arizona. These "cartwheels" originally came from the fabled Comstock Lode at Virginia City, Nevada: they are steeped in the history of the Old West. (The later-date issues of 1889, 1890, 1891, 1892 and 1893 Carson coins are too expensive for our rare coin retirement portfolio, though they would make splendid additions if you want to price average).

Carson City, Nevada was an unlikely site for a United States Mint. A frontier town located near Lake Tahoe, not far from the border of California, and only a couple of hundred miles overland from San Francisco, it was a raucous and violent place a century and a quarter ago. The key to its success was that it was close to Virginia City—site of the fabulous Comstock Lode of silver and gold—and that Carson City was Nevada's capital when it entered the Union in 1861.

A mint for Carson City became the dream of Abraham Curry, a transplanted New Yorker turned real estate promoter, who sought to use it to coin into money the deposits from prospectors Peter O'Riley, Patrick McLaughlin and Henry Comstock, and the thousands of others who flocked westward to exploit the Comstock Lode.

After years of negotiation, a mint was opened in 1870, two years before the current state capitol building was completed—though both are of the same rough-hewn style associated with frontier conditions.

Coins from the Carson City Mint all bear a "CC" mintmark—the only mint to use two letters. The city itself was named for Kit Carson, the famous scout, and like the mint, was built as part of a boom town ruled by mining interests.

The government purchased the land from Abraham Curry for $80,000, and by September, 1866, the cornerstone was laid to start construction. Funding ran out and Curry journeyed from Cal-

A photograph of Virginia City, Nevada in 1878

ifornia to Washington D.C. around Cape Horn by steamer to secure additional funding.

In his *Annual Report of the Director of the Mint* for 1869,
James Pollock wrote to Treasury Secretary George Boutwell that the
"branch mint at Carson City, Nevada is rapidly approaching completion," but days before the scheduled opening, an earthquake
flattened most of the town. The mint, a brick fortress, survived, and
minting operations commenced January 8, 1870.

Located twenty-one miles down the track of the Virginia &
Truckee Railroad from the Comstock Lode mines, ore was sent to
the mint daily for refinement into double eagle $20 gold pieces,
and silver dollars.

Though the free coinage of silver had ended with the passage of the Coinage Act of 1873, the Bland-Allison Act forced the
resumption of silver dollar production, and the Carson City Mint
turned them out by the bag-full. Bags of the Carson City silver dollars were struck at the mint on the presses that had been sent from
Philadelphia to San Francisco by boat around Cape Horn, and
then trucked over land by wagon.

By the end of the 1880s, the Carson Mint had grown expensive to operate for the amount of bullion that was refined, and
the coinage that was struck. Operational costs were $150,476.11
in 1892 (tens of millions in today's dollars), and the government
had little revenue to show for it. The mint finally closed its doors
in 1893.

As the West became civilized, America moved away from
the use of the bulky silver dollars. After the Carson City Mint
closed, the coins were lost in the vaults of the Treasury Department in Washington, virtually forgotten, even as the price of silver
rose and 1903-O silver dollar hoards were discovered. When they
were finally found, the government had the good sense to figure
out that there were 2.9 million silver dollar coins with a value far
above the face value, and set about trying to find a means of selling them.

The government sought the advice of luminaries such as
Edward Rochette, then editor of *The Numismatist,* later executive
director, and finally president of the American Numismatic Asso-

ciation; Margo Russell, editor of *Coin World*; LeRoy Van Allen; Debbie Duke Swann of the U.S. Mint and others. Their unanimous conclusion: sell them, and do it lottery-style to give a fair opportunity to all who wanted to acquire these rare, historic reminders of the Old West.

Here are a half dozen reasons why the Carson City silver dollars ought to be part of your rare coin retirement planning today:

- The mintages are moderate. The 1878-CC has 2.12 million; the 1879-CC some 756,000; 1880-CC is 591,000; 1881-CC is 296,000, 1882-CC is 1.13 million, 1884-CC is 1.2 million; 1885-CC is 228,000—all relatively scarce. More typical mintages: 1884-P at 14 million, 1884-O at 9.1 million and 1884-S and 3.2 million.

- There is a natural charm to coins that were produced in the Old West. These coins are heavily promoted among telemarketers. They are always in demand.

- Silver dollars are among the most widely collected of series. The "Grey Sheet" (*The Coin Dealer Newsletter*) started printing weekly prices of all silver dollar sales as early as 1963. They still do not list all coins by date and mintmark—many are listed by type—but silver dollars are listed by both date and mintmark.

- Trend lines consistently have favored silver dollars. The Carson City dollars are at a modern historic low and are likely to move in the next market push.

- There are numerous mint errors and varieties among the Carson City dollars that are also highly collected, but not often studied. It's a clear opportunity to pick a winner and get a bonus on top of it.

- The "short" set can have the last years added to it easily enough. These coins include the 1889-CC through 1893-CC, though the 1889-CC is an expensive coin when in superior condition.

- These coins are 1½ inches in diameter, large, and quite beautiful—easily suitable for display as well as long-term holding.

These reasons were valid then, also. The result was that legislation was introduced, and with the passage of the One Bank Holding Company Act of 1970, the stage was set for sale of the coins by the General Services Administration, the government's selling arm. After some false starts, the government was in the business of selling rare coins for a nice profit by October, 1972.

Arthur Sampson, director of the GSA, announced the sale at a packed Washington press conference that brought out the print media like *Time* and *Newsweek*, as well as the daily press and television. There was something exciting about the buried treasure that had been discovered in guarded vaults.

GSA's sales techniques bordered on hucksterism. "Their CC mint mark makes them real collector's items, because CC produces are the only U.S. coins 'with a double mint mark'; they are 'an extraordinary value' because they are uncirculated. . . . They are 'genuine nineteenth century coins,'" the promotional literature said. The government then went on to say that "The value of these coins is high since the demand is great" and therefore they are "excellent for investments or gifts."

Well, Uncle Sam was right, though things didn't quite go as originally planned. The government had a convoluted purchasing plan with a minimum bid, and the opportunity for those who wanted one of the rarities that were identified by date and mintmark to pay even more.

Holdings by the government were so substantial that in some cases, such as the 1883-CC, about 62 percent of the total mintage of 1.204 million was still held by the government and ultimately disposed of at the GSA sales between 1972 and 1980. Because of the substantial quantities, the GSA offerings did not initially sell out, and the government stopped its program; but in 1979-80 a determination was made to eliminate the remaining coins altogether with a final series of sales. The series was oversubscribed beyond words.

Some 2.5 million pieces had already been sold, and of the 400,000 pieces left, the government's own press release tells the tale: "I'm sorry," said GSA Commissioner Roy Markon, "we didn't have the more than 5 million coins necessary to satisfy the demand of the American people." (There were 2.9 million silver dollars all told). "Stampede . . . is the only word that adequately describes the opening days of the sale." Markon told his audience "that recent estimates show the government needed an inventory of 5 million of the historic coins to fulfill more than 400,000 orders submitted."

For your rare coin retirement, consider these eight coins: 1878-CC (MS-63, $82), 1879-CC (VF, $100), 1880-CC (MS-60, $130), 1881-CC (MS-60, $143), 1882-CC (MS-64, $76), 1883-CC (MS-64, $76), 1884-CC (MS-64 $76), 1885-CC (AU-50, $155). The average price is about $104 for coins that are chocked with history, good price advances, and the likelihood for a good future.

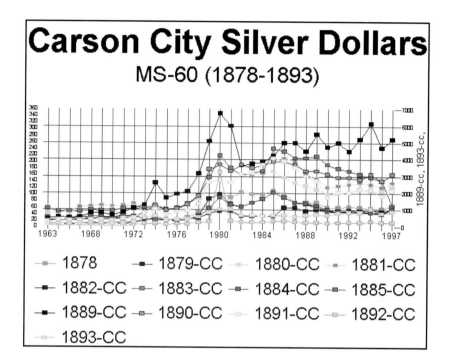

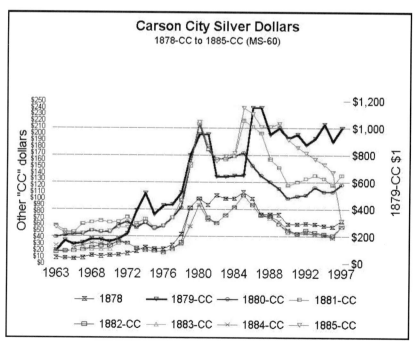

Indian Head Cents
(1900-1909)
Uncirculated (MS-65 $50)
Proof (Proof-64) ($95)

From 1859 until 1909, the one cent coin that circulated throughout America was the Indian Head cent—a misnomer, but one that has stuck to this day. Tens of millions of them were produced, nearly all of which (except those minted in 1908 and 1909) were manufactured at the Philadelphia Mint. Nearly all of these (except for a couple of thousand pieces) began their existence as uncirculated coins, but today, nearly all of them are circulated.

I have a particular fondness for Indian Head cents. This is due in part to the fact that in 1960, I found a circulated one—a well-worn 1906—in pocket change. It started my interest in collecting coins, a hobby that has lasted a lifetime.

James B. Longacre was the designer of the coin, which replaced the Flying Eagle cent, whose duration in circulation was just a little over one and a half years. It was the replacement for the older style large cent that had circulated from the time the mint was founded until 1857, when it could not hold its value as currency against its value as copper.

As legend has it, Sarah Longacre, the chief engraver's daughter, served as the model for the Indian princess whose portrait occupies the one cent coin. Evidently, a group of Native Americans visited the Philadelphia Mint as part of a larger delegation, and one bestowed a bonnet upon Sarah; her father made a sketch of the event, and it subsequently became the Indian Head

43

cent. Whether a legend or a true story, Liberty as she appears has decidedly Anglo features, rather than the high cheekbones often associated with the American Indian.

Cornelius Vermeule, the noted scholar of numismatic design, has demonstrated conclusively that Longacre was fascinated with Indian bonnets a good five years before the Indian Head cent made its appearance. He suggests that the portrait is of a mature woman, rather than a young girl. What is clear is that the design captured the popular imagination at the time. It was the first design that was truly American, rather than yet another example of classical Roman or Greek design.

If you are willing to accept virtually any condition, you could probably purchase any coin in the series for your rare coin retirement portfolio (except for the 1877, which is still scarce and well over the budget of our rare coin retirement portfolio). However, what makes more sense is to purchase the uncirculated and proof coins of the years around the turn of the century. The mintage of each is approximately the same and in terms of availability, they still remain strikingly common, though increasingly scarce.

Proofs from 1890 forward average about 2,000 coins (the high figure is 1890 with 2,740 coins; the lowest is 1908 with 1,620 specimens). In proof-64 condition, these Indian Head cents average about $95 apiece.

Mintages for the uncirculated specimens are more complicated. The most common by far is the 1907. The 1894 uncirculated is many times more rare than the proof, since only 16.7 million pieces were made (typical mintages for the period were around 40 million pieces) and very few of these coins have survived in uncirculated condition. A nice MS-65 specimen should run about $50; the price is much higher for red, brown or red copper cent specimens.

Indian Head cents have had peaks and valleys in popularity and prices have fluctuated along with collector interest. They are due for a rise, particularly in the better-graded material, in part because copper simply does not wear well and preserving its patina, or natural sheen, becomes more difficult as time goes by.

Indian Head Cents 1900-1909 (MS-65 and Proof-64)
Photo Credit: Numismatic News/Krause Publications

The Indian Head cent makes a nice type coin but also a nice collection in and of itself. With the exception of just a couple of coins, most still remain moderately priced: within the realm that a collector can hope to acquire without a frenetic search getting in the way of enjoyment.

Coins in your rare coin retirement plan need to have room for growth. In this case, it will be to return to levels achieved in earlier years when Indian Head cents were more appreciated. While you are acquiring this rare coin retirement portfolio, all of these coins will become at least a century old, an important demarcation in the way some items are priced. Given this coin's history, it is likely that this will happen over the next several years, making this series prime for inclusion in your portfolio.

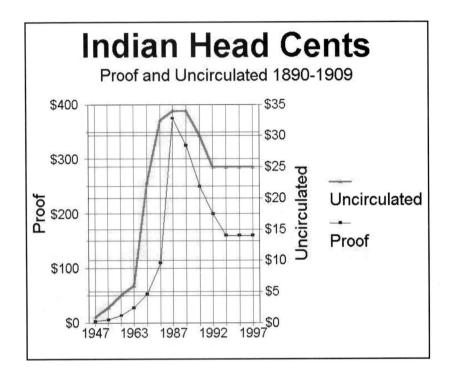

1997 Platinum Tenth of an Ounce Bullion Coin

In 1997, America added its first new bullion coin since 1986, and its first new series of denominations in over a century. A $100 platinum bullion coin (one ounce) joined an array of half ounce, quarter ounce and tenth ounce coins—all featuring a stirring portrait of the Statue of Liberty with a reverse of a soaring eagle.

"The eagle soars!" exclaimed Philip Diehl, director of the United States Mint, at the May 30 West Point Mint ceremony when the first Platinum Eagle was struck.

Although any of these coins could be part of your rare coin retirement portfolio, the tenth of an ounce neatly fits within the parameters that we have established for planning *your* rare coin retirement. The coin has a face value of $10 and sells for under $100 (a deliberate marketing effort by the mint) and has a very modest mintage (maximum of 38,000 pieces).

Platinum has a 250 year history of coinage; the first American platinum pattern was produced around the year 1814. As the Platinum Eagle was being produced, the premium between platinum and gold had increased above historic highs to 25 percent, or more, but that's not the reason why the tenth of ounce proof Eagle belongs in your rare coin retirement collection.

Here are some compelling reasons:

- It is the first U.S. $10 denomination issued as a regular legal tender coin in a metal other than gold.

- It has low mintage for a tenth ounce proof bullion coin.

- It is the first U.S. coin since 1792 whose weight, size, and design has been chosen by the secretary of the Treasury, not Congress—as Congress itself directed.

- They are the first authorized legal tender platinum coins produced by the United States Mint.

- It is the first coin series whose denominations have been chosen by the secretary of the Treasury.

- It is the first coin authorized to "meet competition" of other foreign bullion products.

- It is the first coin produced where all inscriptions are determined by the secretary of the Treasury, not Congress or prior legal requirements.

- It is the first U.S. coin, ever, to have the dollar sign declaring its value.

First of what will soon be a series of issues (tenth, quarter, half, and one ounce) and new denominations ($10, $25, $50 and $100), the new platinum coinage will initially be available as proof issues, with bullion circulation strikes to follow.

To put the new bullion coins in a historic context, gold and silver have been mined since antiquity, and coins from them have been produced for over 2,000 years. By contrast, platinum has a history that is now only 450 years old. It was discovered by Italian scientist Julius Scaliger in 1557, but large quantities of platinum were not available until about 1750, after the Spaniards found platinum in Peru. They named it platinum from their word "plata," which means silver, as a way of describing the grayish color of the metal. Miners frequently refer to it as white gold because it can be found in beds of gold-bearing sand.

Numismatic use of the metal swiftly followed. A platinum medal was produced by Spain commemorating the discovery of the metal in large alluvial quanitites. Coining of platinum began in

1997 Platinum 1/10th Ounce Bullion Coin
Photo Credit: Numismatic News/Krause Publications

1763 using dies normally used for the Columbian 8 escudo gold coin, and continued through 1819.

Chile, Bolivia, Peru and Spain also made unsuccessful attempts at issuing platinum coinage. Spain produced at least thirteen varieties of patterns between 1776 and 1904, all in platinum. The Edwards Metcalf collection had no fewer than 75 different lots of platinum coins, some of them gilt, all struck by Spain. They start with an 8 escudos of Charles III, dated 1786 and mintmarked Madrid-DV, and include issues of Charles IV, Isabella II, Alphonso XII and Maria Christina, Regent (1894). Even into the 1960s, there were new discoveries of platinum coinage issues. In 1962, dealer Jerry Cohen discovered a platinum 1867 10 escudo piece (before then, the only known specimens were dated either 1866 or 1868).

Russia regularly issued platinum coinage for circulation from 1828-1845 in the 3, 6 and 12 ruble denominations. Mintages for the 3 ruble coins of the 1830's shows how well accepted the coin was in Russia: more than 106,000 pieces were produced in 1830, and some 86,500 the following year. In 1832, some 65,767 pieces were produced and in 1842, a total of 145,578 pieces were coined.

To some degree, the tenth ounce platinum coin may have been intended as a jewelry item, but will have a real impact among collectors because of its low mintage and relatively modest price. The sell-out by the United States Mint has not hurt an iota, and, in fact, enhances the overall likelihood of substantial future gains in value for this denomination.

Just making a comparison with the gold bullion coins is interesting. The first of the proofs was issued in 1988 (though the tenth ounce was available as uncirculated in 1986). Total mintage: 143,881.

There will be those who will argue that platinum undersells gold consistently, but that ignores two facts. First, the price of platinum far exceeds the price of gold today (the margin is about $100 an ounce, a spread of about 25 percent); second, collectors look for low mintages, regardless of metal composition.

A good case may be made that because platinum is a precious metal, the tenth ounce proof coin is one of the brightest spots in overall investment potential—and should be a valuable addition to your rare coin retirement.

Thomas Jefferson
Commemorative Dollar
(Uncirculated, $31)

On April 13, 1994, the 251st anniversary of his birth, America's first true Renaissance man, Thomas Jefferson, was honored with a new commemorative dollar coin in impressive ceremonies held at Monticello. The new coin bears an unusual, little-remembered portrait of Jefferson that is arresting in style and design, as well as a distinctive frontal view of Monticello. It sold out almost immediately in uncirculated (266,927 pieces) and proof (about 323,000 pieces). The coin is unusual in that it was issued a year after the 250th anniversary of Jefferson's birth, but collectors rarely look at that aspect of commemoratives—especially since it bears a 1993 date.

The uncirculated coin has strong legs, and already has a price 10 percent above its issue price of $27. Its future, as you plan your rare coin retirement is, therefore, bright. An appealing, historic subject matter (Jefferson), an arresting design and sufficient quantity to allow for a market to be made, make this coin a valuable investment.

Jefferson had diverse knowledge in virtually every field: coinage, architecture, mathematics, history, even design. He spoke several Native American dialects, as well as Latin, Greek, Italian, French, German and Anglo-Saxon. Small wonder that, in 1962, when President and Mrs. Kennedy held a dinner at the White House honoring Nobel prize laureates, the dinner remarks made by Kennedy on the third president included the observation,

Thomas Jefferson Dollar

"I think this is the most extraordinary collection of talent, of human knowledge, that has ever been gathered together at the White House, with the possible exception of when Thomas Jefferson dined alone."

Born April 2, 1743, on the old style calendar (April 13 on the modern calendar), he began a lifetime preoccupation with the House of the Little Mountain (Monticello) when he was elected to the House of Burgesses in Virginia. For some 40 years, between 1769 and 1809, he was constantly involved in building, and enlarging the mountain top home where "all my wishes end [and] where I hope my days will end, at Monticello."

Work began on the mansion in 1767, and continued irregularly, but more aggressively after his marriage to Martha Wayles Skelton, a wealthy widow, in 1772. Still, Jefferson's long absences, in the Burgess, as Governor of Virginia, as a diplomat abroad, and in service of his state and nation, precluded the supervision that he wanted as the architect.

Jefferson's Monticello is familiar to even a school child because of its depiction on the 5-cent piece. It appears to be a two story building with a dome. The dome, after the Temple of Vesta design by Italian architect Andrea Palladio, is a distinctive feature; but the building's height is a deceptive optical illusion.

All this played out on the eventual design of the commemorative coin. First of the issues to be resolved was which portrait of Jefferson was to be used. In one version Jefferson was shown in colonial-style garb and dress, in the other he was dressed in a far different style. Each design was based on a known portrait of Jefferson.

There are but twenty-six live portraits of Jefferson (not including silhouettes) known to have been done during his lifetime. The Houdon marble sculpture of Jefferson, whose stirring likeness is reproduced on the Jefferson 5-cent piece, was purchased from the sculptor by Jefferson in France for 1,000 Livres on July 3, 1789. This was hardly Jefferson's favorite. He preferred one done in his later years, in June of 1805 (when he was sixty-two) by the artist Gilbert Stuart, a celebrated portraitist.

The mint commented that "a depiction of Jefferson in a frock coat and pigtail would be more familiar to the American public due to its use on the Jefferson nickel," but decided against using it for the new coin on grounds of marketability. (The mint had recently issued four coins depicting men in period clothing and hairstyles). In the end, the sketch prepared was based on Houdon's sculpture showing Jefferson as a mature man of forty-six years of age.

On January 20, 1994, the Citizens Advisory Committee, of which I was a member, met to discuss proposed portraiture design. Although the portrait of Jefferson had come under criticism, I found it attractive almost immediately. I sent a fax to my fellow committee members stating that "Given this as a choice, the Jefferson portrait utilized (which my law partner [Teri Towe] immediately recognized as coming from the portrait located at Harvard, a copy of which, he advises me, is at the State Department,) is arresting. It is similar in style to that of Elizabeth Jones for the Olympic $5 gold piece (Nike) and is Greek in culture and depth. It is, in a word, beautiful." The result was a coin that may well redefine the way that Americans think of their nation's third president. Certainly, the James Ferrell rendering, viewed at the Philadelphia Mint in February, 1994, is a beautiful, artistic, sensitive, and exquisitely detailed portrait.

With only a few years since its release, it is difficult to predict this coin's future pricing, but it seems fair to say that the relatively low mintage and a sell out by the mint—which other commemorative coins cannot boast—will go a long way towards effecting price increases in the future, and to making these two coins an attractive addition to your rare coin retirement.

Jefferson Nickel
(1938-1965)
P, D, S BU ($130)

Thomas Jefferson was perhaps America's first Renaissance man, so it was altogether fitting that in 1938, a national design contest was held to add his portrait and a version of his home at Monticello to the design of the nickel, replacing the buffalo and Indian that had graced the denomination since 1913.

There never was a question that the design on the nickel would reflect the portrait by Houdon, the great French sculptor whose defining portrait of Jefferson in marble remains one of the greatest expressions of eighteenth-century art in a classical Greco-Roman style.

Monticello, on the reverse side of the coin, proved to be more problematical. Schlag originally did a three-quarters profile that was exquisite, both in its detail and in its depiction of the beauty of Monticello as a building representing colonial Virginia's finest architecture. This design was modified at the insistance of the secretary of the Treasury to a lifeless, two-dimensional design that is so banal, non-descript, and unrecognizable that the name of the building must appear beneath.

Almost from its issuance, it proved popular with collectors and became an economic workhorse of significant mintage and circulation. The nickel remains a coin of importance even today as America moves toward a cash-less society.

Its metallic composition is dominated by copper, which accounts for 75 percent of its content. The remaining 25 percent

Jefferson Nickel 1938-1965
Photo Credit: Numismatic News/Krause Publications

comes from the element from which the denomination got its name when Joseph Wharton of Pennsylvania used his political influence to cause Congress to authorize the new denomination in 1865.

For your rare coin retirement portfolio, a set of Jefferson nickels is a welcome addition since it actually includes a number of scarce, semi-key dates and is an unusual sub set of coins de-marking World War II.

During the second World War, nickel and copper were both in very short supply. Each was a critical war material. Yet, the nickel was more important for war use than for use in commerce. The mint came up with an ingenious solution: add silver and man-ganese—each scarce, but not critical war material—combine them with copper, and use the nickle for shell casings.

As the Jefferson nickel enters is seventh decade, it remains a relatively easy series for the novice or beginning collector to com-plete, though uncirculated sets are becoming more scarce. The graph below shows checkered history of value, with higher prices that have varied from time to time. This is one of the reasons it is included in your rare coin retirement portfolio. Another is that with all the S-mint only issues, there are some genuinely scarce and low mintage coins, not to mention the 1950-D, which at one time was $600 or more per roll in uncirculated condition but now remains, mysteriously, a coin that is widely available for $10 or less.

Today, you also have the opportunity to buy an uncirculated set of Jefferson nickels 1938-1964 for $130; a bargain when you consider that the same set of coins sold for $365 in 1980.

Jefferson nickels minted prior to 1965 have a couple of important key dates in uncirculated condition. These include the 1938-D, the 1939-S, the 1942-D, each of the silver war nickels (56 percent copper, 35 percent silver, 9 percent manganese), and the 1950-D. A general sense of the importance of these items can be gained from considering their mintages. The 1938 is 5.3 million, the 1950-D is 2.6 million, while most of the others fall in between.

These relatively low mintages are another reason these coins are potentially very valuable and are good additions to your rare coin portfolio.

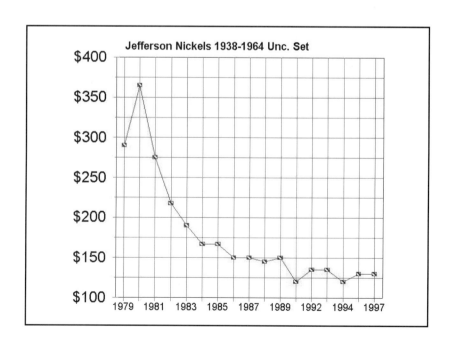

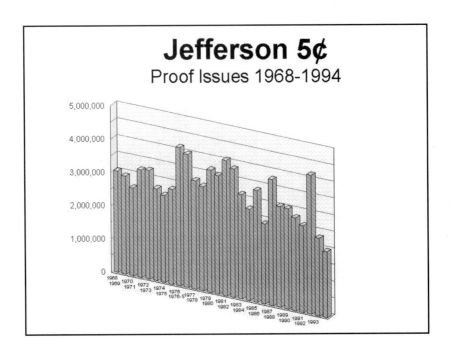

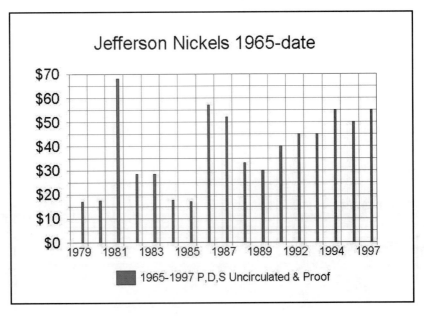

Eisenhower Dollars
1971-1978
($105)

Dwight Eisenhower was so popular that President Harry S. Truman offered to step aside in 1948 if he would become the Democratic nominee for president. The Republican party offered him the nomination in lieu of Thomas E. Dewey that same year. He refused both, preferring instead to become president of Columbia University, as he mustered out of a lifetime of military service and in to civilian life.

But by 1952, his calling was clear and his mandate for change propelled him into the office as the 34th president of United States. Eisenhower's administration, in retrospect, was a mixed bag—yet it laid the foundation for America's rise in the second half of the twentieth century. The stalemate in Asia was ended after Ike went to Korea, fulfilling a campaign promise, but by 1954, American advisors had committed themselves to assist in Vietnam, even after the French failure at Dien Bien Phu. The space race was all but lost as Sputnik was launched by the Soviets in 1957, and by January 1, 1959, Fidel Castro had Havana under bombardment and his regime would soon be in power. On January 20, 1961, Dwight D. Eisenhower, at that time the oldest American President ever to leave the office after two terms stepped into history and retired to Gettysburg.

His remaining years saw him in troubled health, but he was still held in high regard by the country that he had served so long and in so many different capacities. It was predictable that when he died in 1969, there were calls for his numismatic commemoration—and so it was that the One Bank Holding Company Act of 1970 contained a provision calling for the striking of Eisenhower dollars in copper-nickel (for circulation), and in silver (for collectors).

As you plan for your rare coin retirement, the set of Eisenhower dollars in uncirculated and proof should be an important component. One reason can easily be seen on the graph on page 61, which shows how these coins reached their highest value in 1979-80, a level that they are capable of reaching again.

The proof silver Eisenhower dollars had a selling price of $10. To show you how times have surely changed, Treasury Secretary John Connally was widely quoted in the trade press as calling the price 'unconscionable' because of the high profit that the mint made from the sale of the coins.

Design elements on the coin were created by committee: Congress mandated the Eisenhower portrait for the obverse and a commemoration of the first landing of man on the moon on the reverse. There is a certain irony that Eisenhower, on whose watch Sputnik started the space race, was probably the person also responsible for the National Aeronautics and Space Administration (NASA), which was singularly responsible for human kind's greatest reach into space.

The portrait by Chief Engraver Frank Gasparro was drawn both from memory and from a photograph showing Eisenhower at the V-E Day parade in New York City, which Gasparro had at-

Eisenhower Dollar 1971-1978
Photo Credit: Numismatic News/Krause Publications.

tended. Eisenhower, who looked old before his time, looked much the same in 1944 as he did in 1969 at his unique memorialization.

There are two distinctive reverse designs: the lunar landing, and the bicentennial reverse, which in turn, has two distinctive varieties. The first was designed by Dennis R. Williams, a college art student who won the contest with an almost primitive design, and the second had a sharper, more delicate lettering.

The silver proof Eisenhower dollars hold the real key to the series, but their price has slipped far below the original $10 per coin issue price. The silver-clad version (containing .316 troy ounces of silver) has a selling price of about $3, and a high upside potential. The lowest mintage 1973-S (1.013 million coins in proof) is a $13 coin. But the 1.8 million uncirculated version is only a $3 coin; the 1974-S proof is about $3.45 (for a mintage of 1.3 million), while the uncirculated at 1.9 million is around $3. The upside is significant. These thirty-three coins will enhance your rare coin retirement nicely.

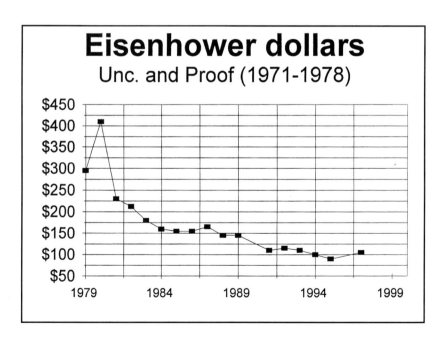

Complete Set of Kennedy Half Dollars 1964-1996

(P, D, S, $300)

Nearly 100 coins comprise a complete set of Kennedy half dollars in uncirculated and proof, at an average of about $3 per coin. That doesn't count the 1974-D double die, which averages around $200, when you can find one. But the set is well within the parameters of a highly collectible set in choice uncirculated and brilliant proof pieces.

Created as a tribute to President John F. Kennedy, who was assassinated November 22, 1963, the new coin made its debut less than three months later. Rather quickly, the new Kennedy half dollar soon took on a life of its own, and as other subsidiary coinage moved into the realm of perpetual shortage because of need and use, the 50-cent piece bearing the portrait of John F. Kennedy was in short supply because its attrition rate in circulation approached 100 percent. Virtually everyone, it seemed, that acquired a Kennedy half dollar put it aside as a memento. There was as much demand for the coin abroad as there was in the United States, as the citizens of the world that Kennedy spoke of in his inaugural address strove to obtain one last commemoration of his presence on earth.

The 1964 Kennedy half was produced in 90 percent silver alloy as were all subsidiary coinage of the era. But the demand proved to be astronomical. Bearing a 1964 date, a total of 277 million pieces were produced by the Philadelphia Mint alone. The Denver Mint produced an additional 156 million pieces. In a single year, the mints produced almost as many half dollars as the Philadelphia, Denver and San Francisco Mints had for the entire Franklin half dollar series in 1948 through 1963.

A total of 100 coins comprise the Kennedy half dollar collection from 1964 until 1994, including a number of different varieties, metallic bases, and compositions. In sheer numerical terms, in its relatively short life, the Kennedy half dollar has had more compositional changes than virtually any other denomination or coin variety.

Starting its life with 90 percent silver as a one year only type, the following year (1965) the Coinage Act changed its composition to silver-clad material with a gross total of 40 percent silver-clad material. This composition continued until passage of the Coinage Act of 1970, which resulted in the creation of the nickel-clad issue of the Kennedy half-dollar. It is essentially this coin that is still produced today.

A modest design change took place during the bicentennial era in 1975 and 1976, when a reverse showing Independence Hall was issued. Designed by Seth Huntington, a collector from Minneapolis, the coin was produced in both copper-nickel clad and silver-clad material.

1970-S Kennedy Half Dollar (Proof)
Photo Credit: Numismatic News/Krause Publications

The original Gasparro reverse was reinstituted in 1977, and is used to this day. In 1994, in addition to the standard copper-nickel clad material, the mint produced a collector's edition manufactured in silver by a mandate of Congress.

Collecting Kennedy half dollars is somewhat of a challenge because so many of the coins were only produced for collectors, and were not intended for circulation. The first of such issues took place in 1970, when the only pieces produced were the 1970-D (found in the mint set of that year) and the 1970-S (found in the proof set).

Important varieties of the Kennedy half dollar widely recognized by collectors include the first year of issue type with two versions: one with "accented" or accentuated hair (of which between 100,000 and 200,000 proofs were made from between fifty to sixty coin dies, early in the production cycle), various versions that fail to have the initials FG (for the engraver, Frank Gasparro) on the reverse (such as the 1972 half from Denver Mint and the 1982 half from Philadelphia and Denver Mints), and proof errors involving the 1979 "S" Mint, which is either clear or filled.

Even nearly 40 years after his assassination, and despite the revelations that he was all too human and fallible, John F. Kennedy remains the subject of legend, his assassination the subject of controversy, and his half dollar one of the world's most widely collected coins.

1970-D Kennedy Half Dollar (Unc.)
Photo Credit: Numismatic News/Krause Publications

An absurd example of the upside potential of these coins is that nine common-date Kennedy half dollars with a total face value of $4.50 and a silver value of less than $20, all of them obviously circulated, but otherwise highly desirable as collector's items, brought nearly $9,000 at a public auction conducted by Sotheby's in New York City in the Spring of 1997. Regular Kennedy half dollars routinely sell for less than $10 apiece, even in gem condition. The reason that these were so special was that each of the coins was part of the estate of Jacqueline Bouvier Kennedy Onassis, the former first lady and widow of John F. Kennedy.

When the dust settled, the Kennedy half dollars looked downright cheap, indeed, the bargain of the highly publicized sale, where virtually everything sold for far more than its catalog estimate.

1989-D Congressional Half Dollar

(Uncirculated, $12)

Contemporary commemorative silver dollars are ripe candidates for helping to plan your rare coin retirement. Despite the criticism that they are contrived and overpriced when issued, history shows that collectors have a short memory.

Each of the problems or complaints associated with modern commemorative coin issues were the problems and complaints during the heyday of earlier commemorative coins a half century ago. They were issued shamelessly for profit, often without reason. Why else would the Cincinnati Music Center commemorative of 1936 (5,005 pieces from the mints at Philadelphia, Denver and San Francisco) have the portrait of Stephen Foster? The anniversary celebrated has no relationship to Foster, save that both were involved with sharps, flats, and music.

A half century ago, Congress was warned about exploitation of the coinage system and issuance of commemorative coinage in a wasteful and wanton manner. The result was the termination of commemorative issues in 1954, which lasted two generations.

What is instructive and important as you plan for your rare coin retirement, is to consider what these improbable coins have become a generation or two later: they are important collectibles that the contemporary collector seeks to acquire without regard to the underlying negative history. Forgotten in the byways of time are the controversies; what remains is a legal tender coin that, like those from generations before it, are sought eagerly by collectors, who only look upon it as a rare, low-mintage coin.

What are almost always significant with such coins are the overall mintage, the method of strike (circulation strike or proof), the condition, and the theme (which most collectors don't pay a lot of attention to, but which some non-collector purchasers do).

Among contemporary issues, some seem likely to have more legs than others. The Congressional bicentennial dollar, authorized for 1989 issuance, is one of these coins. The bicentennial half dollar, also minted at Denver, is another reasonable candidate at $10.50. When it was issued, the 1989-D uncirculated Congress commemorative silver dollar (mintage 135,203) had a lower mintage than any silver dollar produced during the twentieth century (including Morgan, Peace, Eisenhower and Anthony series). Even when considering the entire Morgan silver dollar series dating to 1878, only three coins have a lower mintage: the 1895 (proof only issue), 1893-S and 1894. Each of these coins is rare and pricey, whereas the Congressional silver dollar is still a coin that you could purchase eight or nine of and be within your portfolio budget of $100 per item.

A total of three million Congressional half dollars were authorized, and just 931,640 were struck. The overwhelming majority of these (767,897) were produced as proofs, while the

1989-D Congressional Half Dollar (Unc.)
Photo Credit: Numismatic News/Krause Publications

remaining 163,000 (17.6 percent of the total) are uncirculated. Attractively designed, with the Mace of the House on the reverse, and the Statue of Freedom atop the Capitol Dome on the obverse, the coin originally sold for $25 as a proof, $23 as uncirculated.

There are other modern commemorative silver dollars with lower mintages, but this one has "legs" in a significant way: it marks a bicentennial anniversary, something that is not at all contrived. While that may not matter to the long-term collector, it helps bolster the price now.

While many true collectors prefer the proof to the uncirculated issue, and because of this the mintage numbers tilt overwhelmingly toward the proof, and away from the circulation strike, it is mintage and survivability that ultimately determine whether or not a coin is a good investment over time. That is precisely what the uncirculated Congressional bicentennial dollar has going for it. It is instructive to consider the 1926 sesquicentennial issue, of which 141,120 were left after meltings by the mint. Some seventy years later, the coin's value is between $150 and several thousand dollars (depending on the actual assigned grade or condition). Even the 1920 Pilgrim tercentenary (152,112 pieces left after meltings), the price range for an uncirculated coin ranges from $75 to $500 or more.

No one can predict whether that is what is in store for the Congressional bicentennial coin, but that is at least one possibility—and a good reason to include multiple examples in your rare coin retirement plan.

1994 American Numismatic Association Commemorative Platinum Coin
(Turks & Caicos, $50)

Turks and Caicos, a British colony in the West Indies, not far from the Bahamas, has a population of about 10,000. Sometimes it appears that there are almost as many commemorative coins from this colony as people living there. As a Crown Colony, Turks and Caicos is not self-governing. The decisions of its local legislature must be given royal ascent, and even coin designs are approved at Whitehall, the British equivalent to the Department of State.

Foreign coinage, including that of Turks and Caicos, is under-appreciated by many coin collectors, as well as many who invest in the field. But it is an area that can only grow because of that undervaluation.

Many years ago, when John Jay Pittman was building his collection, he hit a wall with certain U.S. coins because of cost, and expanded his horizon to include foreign coins. For the most part, he was able to acquire major foreign rarities at a fraction of what a comparable American coin would have cost. At the time of his death in 1996, his world coin collection was among the finest ever assembled, and certainly was the most comprehensive single holding of Canadian, Cuban, Philippine, Japanese, Mexican and South African coinages ever assembled by one person.

The very things that attracted Pittman to foreign coin collecting, should attract you to some foreign coins that ought to be included in your rare coin retirement. That inevitably necessitates a broader look at some series, and countries that previously may have been viewed as less than interesting.

In 1993, the twenty-fifth anniversary the following year of the landing of Apollo 11 was commemorated with a silver proof 20 crown piece (selling for $45 and catalogued Krause/Mishler 142). However, a more interesting item for inclusion in your rare coin portfolio would be a coin for fun, the 1994 first lunar landing that salutes coin collecting and the American Numismatic Association (Krause/Mishler 132) 10,000 of which were struck.

For rare coin retirement purposes, it is best not to include the 10,000 mintage of the copper-nickel space commemorative, except for novelty purposes. But the platinum version of this distinctive coin is most worthy of consideration. Fewer than 100 pieces were produced in a tenth ounce denomination that is about the size of an American dime. Her Majesty, Queen Elizabeth II, appears on obverse using a traditional portrait by Raphael Maklouf, which adorns all coinage of the commonwealth, and that of Britain itself. The portrait shows H.M. Queen Elizabeth in a mature portrait, as contrasted with the youthful version that was used when she ascended the throne in 1952. The reverse is designed by noted sculptor, Don Everhart II, and depicts an astronaut on the lunar surface and includes the phrase, "salute to coin collecting." Everhart is an award-winning designer who produces medals and coins. This is truly a rare opportunity to acquire a piece of sculpture that is at the same time a collectible with future value.

Many Turks & Caicos issues of 5,000 pieces or more are common, relatively speaking, and are fully capable of being absorbed into the marketplace. These coins are much smaller in mintage and in size. A tenth of a crown denomination, weighing 3.11 grams and made of .9995 platinum, contains a tenth of an ounce of platinum and originally sold for $50. The sole source of this coin was the American Numismatic Association Enterprise

Fund. Today, ANA's enterprise is not the sole source for the coins. There is a thriving secondary market. As platinum grows as a contemporary precious metal for coinage, the value of the original coin has surpassed the issue price, and is making a secondary market nicely on its own.

Lincoln Cent Collection
1934-1958
(BU, $60)

There is no question that Lincoln cents from 1934 to 1958 are scarce and are becoming increasingly so. From the authorization of the 1-cent coin in 1793 until 1958, a total of about 28 billion 1-cent coins were produced. Compared to the Lincoln Memorial cent, of which more than 350 billion have been produced since 1959, the 'wheaties' (after the sheath on the reverse) are downright scarce.

With the cent threatened with extinction, it seemed natural for the price to rise, as indeed it did in 1979, when the price topped $200 for the set. Since then, it has gone into a genteel decline, perhaps because it is a tough series to collect individually—though at the present time, you can purchase it at the bargain price of a mere $60. Here's why: there are a number of key and semi-key coins in uncirculated condition, (1934-D, 1935-D, 1936-S, 1938-S, 1939-D, 1942-S and 1949-S), which together more than make up the cost of the overall set. The set, of course, does not comprise a 1955 double die, which is rare and too expensive, but has plenty of overall growth opportunity. For the real enthusiast, there's even the possibility of going back to 1909 and filling in on a coin-by-coin basis and building a real collection.

Victor David Brenner, the great twentieth-century sculptor, should be given credit for a job well done. His design came at the express invitation of President Theodore Roosevelt. President Roo-

Lincoln Cent 1934-1958 (Unc.)
Photo Credit: Numismatic News/Krause Publications

sevelt himself approved the designs in February, 1909, after conferring with the mint director at the White House.

Brenner's design of Abraham Lincoln is at once artistic and sensitive, and conveys the moodiness of the sixteenth president of the United States, as well as the majesty of his greatness. Although it would be another generation before Daniel Chester French would sculpt Lincoln and make him truly larger than life with the Lincoln Memorial, the Brenner portrait is a good start, and even today defines the way that we think of Lincoln.

The reason that 1934 coin has been chosen for your collection (from some twenty-five years of coinage) is purely arbitrary. It is certainly possible to go earlier than 1934—but the coins start to become individually expensive. Besides, the *Coin Dealer*

Newsletter gives quotes for that collection, and also prices for brillian uncirculated cent rolls from 1934 to the present.

What is also nice about including this in your are coin retirement plan is that you can add other cent pieces and round out the set, if that is your inclination. There are some real rarities (the 1909-S VDB, 1914-D, 1922-P) but most of the other coins are really quite affordable. Even a low mintage coin like the 1924-D (mintage just 2.5 million pieces) is available in MS-63 condition at moderate prices of a couple of hundred dollars.

There is considerable upside potential to the 1934-1958 series as well. Lincoln cents have historically been the most popularly collected coins. One reason is that so many people began coin collecting with this denomination. Many of those coins were in fact taken from pocket change as late as the mid 1960's, when it was still possible to find a well-worn example of a key date in circulation.

What's exciting about a $60 set of Lincolns is that the upward potential is so substantial. The 1934-D with a mintage of 28 million, is priced in the *Guide Book* at $16 in MS-60—a quarter of the value of the overall set. The 1935-S in MS-60 is listed there at $8.

From the perspective of someone acquiring the Lincoln Memorial set (some of which can still be obtained from circulation quite easily), it is a natural progression to take the next step back in mintage date—hence the likely continued future popularity of this series.

Not typically included in this set, but probably includible to comprise its own collection, would be the proof-issue cents covering the same period. They are priced too high collectively, but individually could easily be nice additions to a overall rare coin retirement package.

Overall, the Lincoln cent mini-series looks like a strong candidate for your rare coin retirement—one that can grow as you plan for tomorrow.

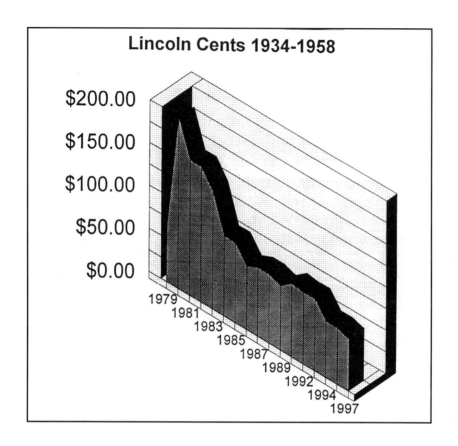

Lincoln Memorial Cent
(1959-D through 1997-P, D, S)
($120)

Although it is a government building, it is one of the most awe-inspiring places. The pilgrimage to it is made each year by millions of people, most of whom pay their respects with awed silence and the respect accorded a man who, while living, was larger than life. In death he has assumed gigantic proportions. The man is Abraham Lincoln, the place is the Lincoln Memorial, and each is commemorated on the 1-cent piece that has now been circulating for nearly a half century.

The man who saved the Union during the four long, hard years when the nation suffered through the Civil War became the subject of American coinage in the year of the centennial of his birth, 1909. To mark the sesquicentennial, the reverse side was changed and the Lincoln Memorial in Washington was added.

Victor David Brenner, whose initials are found on the 1909 cent, and again at the shoulder of the cent in 1918 and afterwards, is the sculptor for the obverse. The reverse was crafted by an assistant sculptor who later became the chief engraver of the United States, Frank Gasparro.

After circulating for nearly two generations the Lincoln Memorial cent has finally come of age, and in the process it makes for exciting collecting for those seeking the challenge of finding coins that have some degree of rarity, but that can still be found in circulation.

More than 350 billion Lincoln Memorial cents have been coined since its introduction on January 2, 1959. The coin is a popular one, and in a May 23, 1990 survey by the Gallup polling organization, 62 percent of all Americans favored the continued use of the coin.

The original design for the Lincoln Memorial cent by Frank Gasparro was selected from a group of twenty-three models that the engraving staff of the mint had been asked to present for consideration. The initial sketch was sent to the Fine Arts Commission for review on May 18, 1958. It copied the style of the nickel by stating the name of the building being commemorated on the coin itself. This proved unnecessary because the skilled detail so precise that under minor magnification, the statue of Lincoln can be plainly seen in the center of the building between the columns.

President Eisenhower himself announced the design change on December 20, 1958. A total of twenty-two steps on the memorial's stairway are shown—a use of artistic license, since the actual memorial is the size of a nine-story building with many more steps and is built on the equivalent of land a half-acre in size. The majesty of Daniel Chester French's statue inside, depicting a Lincoln twenty-eight feet tall (if standing), is captured on the small cent. Engraved on the temple wall, on the interior of the edifice, is a simple dedicatory inscription: "In this temple, as in the hearts of the people for

Lincoln Memorial Cent 1959-1997 (Proof) Including S-Mint Proofs
Photo Credit: Numismatic News/Krause Publications

whom he saved the Union, the memory of Abraham Lincoln is enshrined forever."

The outside columns (numbering thirty-six one for each state in the union at the time of Lincoln's presidency) are doric in design and are forty-four feet high. But only a dozen of the exterior columns are visible on the coin itself.

Commencing its existence with the use of standard bronze, the composition of the Lincoln cent changed in 1962 when President Kennedy signed Public Law 89-643, which eliminated tin from the coin mixture. Zinc was added to a 95 percent copper base, which lasted until the 1980's, when copper was entirely eliminated, except as a plating element over a core that is 99.2 percent zinc.

The 1959 Lincoln cent began the series and to some extent defines it. This coin belongs in your rare coin retirement portfolio as do some rarities that are still obtainable from circulation—the 1995 double die cent is an example—and from proof coinage. The 1960 small date cent in proof and the 1970-S small date are two such coins. Starting in 1975 proof-only issues have relatively low mintages of between 2 and 3 million; a high of 4.1 million was produced in 1992. To get a relative idea of the scarcity, the last time that the mint produced 2.5 million cents was in 1924 at the Denver Mint, and the 1924-D is a key coin in the regular Lincoln series.

This is a popular series and one poised for growth. Unlike some other contemporary issues, the overall trend line for this one is in the upward direction. This is a sure winner for your rare coin retirement.

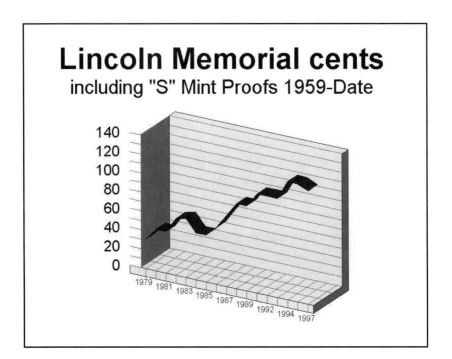

Lincoln Memorial cents
including "S" Mint Proofs 1959-Date

1993 Madison
Commemorative 50¢ Coin
(Uncirculated)

In 1993 the Madison Foundation, acting in concert with the American Numismatic Association to commemorate the bicentennial of the Bill of Rights, sponsored the issue of an extraordinary new collectible struck by the U.S. Mint, and modified with the serial number issued by the sponsoring foundation.

Marketed at a pre-issue price of only $19.95 until October 15, 1993, ($26.95 thereafter) as part of a "Freedom Pack" created by ANA, the coins are unique, distinctive and highly individualized. Only a limited quantity of 9,656 sets were produced. This was only the second time since commemoratives were first authorized in 1892 that a sponsoring organization has altered a numismatic product and authorized its issuance to the public. The last time was in 1925, when Stone Mountain commemorative half dollars were also specially marked.

What makes the Madison Foundation/ANA commemorative so distinctive is that it is both edge-lettered and serially numbered on the coin itself. This creates a distinctive coin design on the third side of the coin: its edge. Edge lettering has been utilized on U.S. coinage since its inception in 1793. It was recently rediscovered as part of regular issue commemorative coinage issued by the U.S. Mint. This specially marked commemorative piece is not issued by the mint, though the coin itself is produced by it.

Marking the edge with the initials JMMFF (James Madison Memorial Fellowship Foundation) and ANA, with a serial number in

*The James Madison Bill of Rights
Commemorative silver half-dollar.*

between, is intended to show the joint nature of the venture, a first in modern times for contemporary commemorative coin issues.

Origins of the marketing idea can be traced to Lewis Larsen, who works for the Madison Foundation and was placed in charge of both shepherding the legislation authorizing the coin through Congress, and later, its marketing. The mission of the program was to raise funds for Madison Foundation scholarships, which are awarded annually to teachers in each of the fifty states to allow them to become year-long fellows in residence in Washington. There, they can study the Constitution as a living document, learn about American law, and later carry this, together with a healthy respect for principles of American government, back to their students.

Since serialization of packaging was nixed by the mint, the ANA decided to find out whether or not a private minting facility could put a serial number on the edge of the coin itself. Silvertowne, of Winchester, Indiana, was eventually chosen to make the modification.

To accomplish the serial number, the edge of the coin needed to be shaved, since it was reeded in conformity with tradition, as opposed to law. Once the edge was ground down, a die was needed to incuse the serial number and the initials of the sponsoring organizations.

Silvertowne's die shop created the markings for the edge, and worked up several production samples. The first was completed on the Thursday before the ANA convention opened in Baltimore in 1993, and was received by the ANA vice president in New York the following day. Admiral Paul Yost, president of the Madison Foundation, spoke of the "investment potential" of these coins, and it is true that the Stone Mountain commemoratives that are serially numbered have a substantially higher value than the regular coin, as does a 1960s counterstamp on the Cleveland issue, done by a local coin club.

No one can predict the future of coin collecting, or any of the modern commemorative products, but on paper, this coin has a number of features that suggest that it could have a greater appeal than some other coins. First, it is an uncirculated silver half dollar, not otherwise singly available. (To acquire it, you had to order it either with the silver dollar, or as part of a three or six coin Madison set). Second, this half dollar uncirculated is of low mintage. Only one million pieces were authorized in the first place, and of some 700,000 regular pieces ordered, more than two-thirds are proofs. So, of the remaining 200,000 pieces in uncirculated condition only a small number will have serial numbers on the edge, as well as the unique imprimatur of both the James Madison Memorial Fellowship Foundation, and the American Numismatic Association.

1903-O Morgan Silver Dollar,
MS-60 ($135)

Few Morgan silver dollars, or any coin for that matter, have a history as interesting and exciting as the 1903 Silver dollar manufactured at the United States Mint in New Orleans, Louisiana.

The coin was struck in steaming New Orelans at the plantation-style mint located in the French Quarter (Vieux Carre), just steps from where riverboat gamblers would use the silver "cartwheels" to ply their trade. Silver was deposited, coined, bagged and stored in the mint that was then in its declining years (it would close as a coining facility forever in 1909). Those that were used went into circulation in the Crescent City and beyond.

Bags of uncirculated silver dollars, packed 1,000 to a sealed bag, were shipped from the New Orleans Mint to the main Treasury building, at Fifteenth and Pennsylvania, NW, Washington, D.C., just across the street from the White House. There they were deposited into the Treasury Department's vault to lay undisturbed for sixty years.

For the collector of 1963, the 1903-0 Silver dollar was a truly rare coin. The "Red Book," actually entitled, *A Guide Book of United States Coins*, then in its sixteenth edition, listed the coin at $1,500 in uncirculated condition. Even contrasted with genuine rarities, the value of the coin was impressive. A 1796 quarter eagle (just 897 pieces struck) was valued at $1,450 in fine condition that year; the 1802 half dime in fine condition was listed at $900; an uncirculated 1909-S Victor David Brenner (VDB) cent was a mere $165, and the 1914-D was $410.

The New Orleans Mint

Today, a 1796 quarter eagle in fine condition is a $10,000 coin; the 1802 half dime is a $20,000 coin in fine-12 condition. The 1909-S VDB cent is $800 in MS-63, and the 1914-D is $1,300.

Another good measure might very well be early, old-time proof sets, such as those contained in the Howard Egolf collection sold by Stack's in 1961. The average price for one of those sets from the early 1900s was about $400. Thus, about three of those proof sets would have equaled the price of a 1903-O silver dollar.

Today, those sets are worth thousands of dollars apiece. A 1901 set that realized $235 in the Egolf sale of 1961 re-sold at the 1976 Stack's ANA sale for $1,700, and was sold again in 1995 at auction for more than $17,000. By contrast, the 1903-0 silver dollar, was worth $135 to $150 in MS-60 uncirculated condition.

What transpired was a Treasury Department practice that became part of numismatic legend in the mid-1960s. Up through the 1960s, silver dollars were still commonly available in banks throughout the country. Tellers set them aside, sometimes for good customers, sometimes for themselves, but the coins were always available as change if requested. All of that changed in 1963, as the price of silver began to move towards a rubicon, of $1.29 an ounce, the price at which it began to pay to melt silver coins for the monetary value.

At Christmas time in 1963, the Treasury cash room vaults opened previously unopened bags of silver dollars and exchanged them one for one for paper money. To the surprise and delight of those on line at the cash room, some of the coins included the 1903-O Morgan dollar in very substantial quantities. If the recipients had kept silent, it is possible that the coins could have been absorbed into the marketplace over a long period of time and this would have increased their value. Human greed and emotion entered the picture however, and in a very short period of time, the previously scarce became relatively common, and the price plummeted from $1,500 to a mere $30 a coin.

Eventually, the market did stabilize and a 1903-O silver dollar today has a value of about $125 in MS-60, and nearly $300 in MS-65 condition.

The MS-60, though a nice coin with a lot of growth potential, is slightly outside the price level of $100, but fits well within the scope of our overall portfolio, since there are so many other coins included that are at a lower price.

For Morgan silver dollars, generally speaking, the minimum grade of acceptability for investment purposes is a MS-60 coin. As one of the most popularly collected series, the 1903-0 is well positioned for future advances, and is a recommended addition to your rare coin retirement portfolio.

1903-O Morgan silver dollar (MS-60)
Photo Credit: Numismatic News/Krause Publications

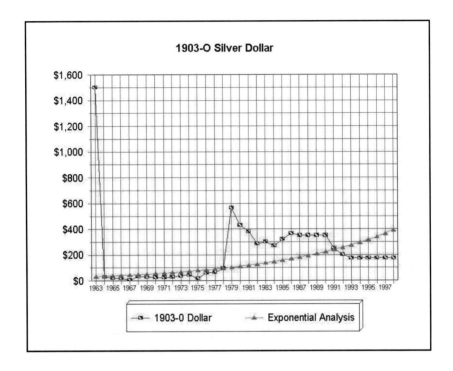

Roosevelt Dime Set
(1946-1997 P, D, S) ($100)

Franklin Delano Roosevelt served as president longer than any other man. At the time of his death on April 12, 1945, he had been president for more than twelve years, guiding America from the darkest days of the Depression, through a near-defeat at Pearl Harbor, and on to victory in Europe and Japan. A generation of people truly thought that the word "president" was an adjective modifying Roosevelt.

FDR is arguably one of the two or three most influential men to have ever held the office of president of the United States. From the start, there was never a doubt that Roosevelt would be honored on the nation's coinage. President Truman was determined to honor his predecessor, as were the American people.

A talented Black artist, Selma Burke, is given credit today for the sketches used for the Roosevelt dime. John Sinnock, chief engraver of the United States Mint, executed the design without giving Burke appropriate credit.

The dime, like the man it honored, was controversial. The obverse contained the initials "JS," which in the period at the beginning of the cold war, were believed by some to be the initials of Joseph Stalin. It got to the point that the mint had to issue a formal denial and explain that John Sinnock, the chief engraver, had placed his initials on the neck's base in accordance with a time-honored custom.

Controversy aside, the dime was a hit from the beginning. Franklin Delano Roosevelt, Jr., the late president's son, announced

Roosevelt Dime Set 1946-1997 (Unc. and Proof)
Photo Credit: Numismatic News/Krause Publications

on national radio hookup from the White House in January, 1946, that the release of the new coin was to coincide with the March of Dimes campaign. The coin replaced the Winged Cap or Mercury dime that had circulated from 1916 to 1945. The Philadelphia, Denver, and San Francisco Mints, and later the West Point facility, were used to make this coin.

Widely collected as a set, the silver coins from 1946 to 1964 have a number of semi-key or scarce dates. Among them are the 1947-S, 1948-S, 1949-S, 1950-S and 1951-S. The 1955-P, D and S are widely seen as 'sleepers,' whose value is still not fully appreciated in the marketplace.

A dozen or so years ago, the late Benjamin Stack (a premier auctioneer associated with Stack's Rare Coin Company in New York) was calling an important sale at which coins were bringing tens of thousands of dollars—many substantially above their estimates. A set of Roosevelt dimes came up on the auction block and started at $50, jumped to $100, and then to $200 as the audience gasped. At $240 the auctioneer stopped the sale in progress and proclaimed to the eager bidders that Stack's retail establishment would furnish prospective bidders with as many sets as they wanted at that price. The price has since fallen, and with it the profit potential locked into the set.

Another interesting feature of the set are the proof-only issues starting with the 1968 issue. Relatively low in overall mintage (4 million and under) these thirty years of issues constitute a significant rarity that can only increase in value in the coming years.

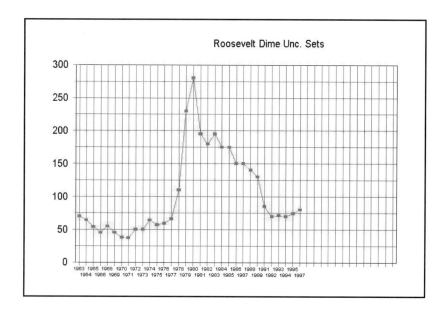

Roosevelt Dimes 1965-1997
(Uncirculated and Proof)

Modern Roosevelt dimes from 1965 to date now number over 100 coins, and that doesn't include the 1982 FDR dime without a mintmark that was produced at the Philadelphia Mint. In fact, the set is now twice the size of the original silver set from 1946-1964. These coins have the same design, and history as the set that began in 1946 to honor Franklin D. Roosevelt. The added part of their story is that until the 1990s, all were without silver, since the coinage of silver was halted by Congress with the passage of the Coinage Act of 1965.

As that series began in 1965 with coins from just the Philadelphia and Denver Mints, no one realized that the set would become popular, nor that it would bear four mintmarks (San Francisco and West Point would be added later). But even with a set of more than a hundred coins, the value is not assured unless there are some key elements present:

- Relative rarity. As of 1997, of 102 coins in the set, fifteen of the coins have mintages of fewer than 3.2 million pieces. A full third of the coins in this set actually have mintages of under five million coins. Want a sample of other dimes in the twentieth century with a mintage that low? Try the 1905-O Barber dime (3.4 million mintage), which today is a $600 coin in uncirculated condition, or consider the 1919-D (9.9 million minted), in 1997 a $400 coin. In the whole Mercury dime series (1916-1945), only seven coins have as small a mintage as these.

- The coin is relatively small with a diameter of just under 18 millimeters. Condition on the proof coins is excellent, with the starting point on nearly all being proof-65 or better.

- A significant part of the mintage is tied up in keeping proof sets available to collectors. To get some of these coins, you have to break up a proof set. That means the available mintage is lower.

- It's an extension of an existing set (Roosevelt dimes, 1946-1964), which is also relatively easy to acquire and complete, and this allows for a complete 150 coin collection.

- The subject matter is not artificial; the coin honors the thirty-second president of the United States.

This series has had its ups and downs, as the graph shows, but the overall trend line is in a steadily upward direction. It also

1996 Roosevelt dime.

has some interesting new coins—the silver proof issues that were specially authorized by Congress. These come from the silver proof sets with the dime, quarter and half dollar, and while there is not yet widespread collectability of this series, the mintages are very low—well under a million pieces—and that is a near mandate for prices to start to rise once the series is discovered.

Quantities are still available, which means that there can be some mass merchandising. which is always desirable in planning for a rare coin retirement because it has the practical effect of helping to be an artificial stimulus to move the demand and price upward. That is simple supply and demand economics. Even an artificial demand with a constant supply that must run down or out, causes a price rise.

The underrated issue is the 1996-W dime, produced at West Point Mint, and made available as an enhancement for customers of annual mint sets only. Here is an uncirculated (not a proof) coin with a very modest mintage, and that suggests that the price could go quickly upward.

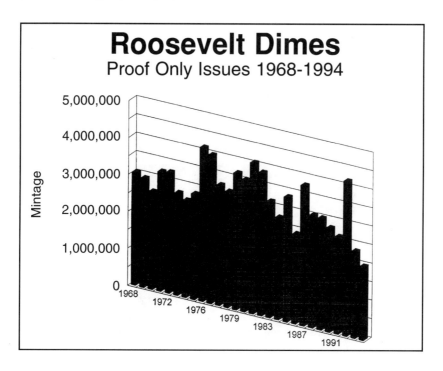

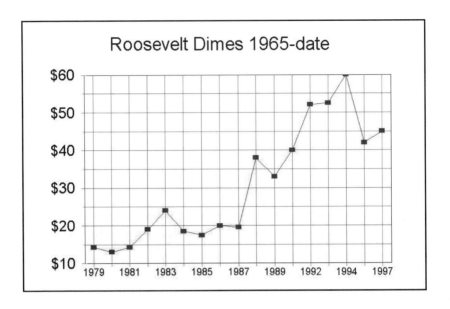

If the collecting instinct really strikes you, it is possible to take the set that you have and upgrade individual coins, so that instead of a proof-67 or MS-66 contemporary dime, you go for a coin near perfection. It will take longer, and cost more, but could well be worth it. Small coins like the dime have fewer detracting marks as a rule. Lacking the bagmarks or scratches, the coins tend to grade better. They look better, have a low mintage, and seem on a fast track to being a winner as you plan your rare coin retirement.

Roosevelt Dime Set 1946-1997 (Unc. and Proof)
Photo Credit: Numismatic News/Krause Publications

1881-S Morgan Silver Dollar
(MS-65) ($65)
(MS-63) ($28)

For a long time, the 1881-S Morgan silver dollar has been cited as a bellwether of rare coin investment, so the piece belongs in your rare coin retirement portfolio even though an 1881 MS-65 Morgan from the San Francisco Mint is one of the most widely available of coins.

Q. David Bowers, one of the most prolific of writers, and a respected dealer, who served as both president of the Professional Numismatists Guild and the American Numismatic Association, recites convincing evidence in his two volume book, *Silver Dollars: A Complete Encyclopedia*, that there are more hoards of this particular date and mintmark than perhaps any other coin. More than 12.7 million pieces were made in San Francisco, and many of them were stored at what was then the "new" San Francisco Mint that survived the 1906 earthquake to become known as the Old Granite Lady.

By the 1960s, the coins had been transferred to Treasury Department vaults in Washington, where they were exchanged for silver certificates, and other coins upon request. In addition, it is evident that many of the coins were stored in the national banking system, which counted silver dollars as part of currency reserves well into the early 1960s.

When the coin market has moved, this is a coin that has parallelled it closely. One reason is that there were such substantial quantities in such superior states of preservation, that

An 1881-S Morgan silver dollar

sellers—particularly telemarketers—had sufficient quantities to be able to really push the coin on investors.

More than 50,000 of these coins have been graded MS-64 by the Professional Coin Grading Service (PCGS); over 30,000 have been termed MS-65. Some of these are no doubt hoard coins from the Redfield dollar holdings (sold by 1976 court order to A-Mark) or the Continental-Illinois Bank quantity that was liquidated in the 1980s by Edward Milas, a Chicago coin dealer associated with Rare Coin Company of America (RARCOA).

What is striking is the graph on page 101 that shows the MS-65 coin superimposed on the MS-63 coin, using differing scales (since the 1881-S as MS-65 is still multiples of the price for one as MS-63). The result is that the MS-63 appears to be the slightly better buy today, and shows that it has advanced more, and picked up more strength than the MS-65 counterpart.

Less than $1 million is tied up in MS-63 silver dollars dated 1881-S; just shy of $2 million is tied up with MS-65 coins of the same date and mintmark. The graph's slopes suggest greater growth for the MS-63 coin, and so you can opt to buy three of them or go for a single example of the MS-65 as you plan your rare coin retirement.

A further word of caution is in order. While I have always viewed the 1881-S as a good market bellwether, there are those who disagree with that view. Q. David Bowers, whose astute observations are nearly universally admired, observes that a "gullible investor might readily believe" that a single coin can determine the movements of a whole market, but a serious collector would not.

My view is that Bowers is correct, that a serious collector would rarely look at a single coin and determine that it is an entire market. But from my perspective, the 1881-S coin's marketability foretells how telemarketers are able to perform in the selling of coins, and how prices generally have held through the years.

But a look at the graph below shows that the 1881-S market, when compared with the Salomon Brothers portfolio used for so long to predict the prices of rare coins, shows that the 1881-S market is more volatile, but that it's higher sweeps and lower dips are more substantial. That is, it broadly predicts what is happening in the market place.

Guarantees are rare, so consider this a strong recommendation. Watch the 1881-S. When it moves, it is likely that it will carry the market with it, or that its movement will be broadly representative of the marketplace as a whole.

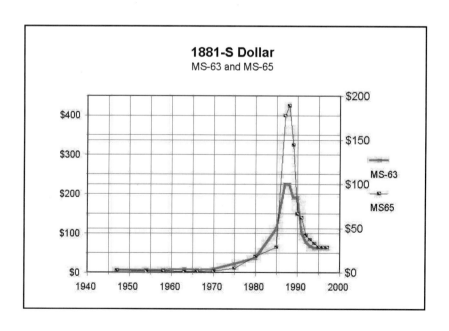

1970-D Kennedy Half Dollar
(uncirculated)

The claim that contemporary coins do not belong in your rare coin retirement portfolio is proved dramatically wrong by the 1970-D half dollar, a 50-cent coin produced at the Denver Mint, especially for collectors.

With just 2.15 million pieces issued, the coin was struck only in mint sets, and was not otherwise intended for circulation. This coin is almost a guaranteed winner, yet few collectors have begun to recognize it, making it a "sleeper" and a bargain.

This marks the first of the modern issues struck just for collectors, and it is a rarity worthy of inclusion in any collection. The coin is needed for any set of Kennedy halves or mint sets to be complete.

What makes it especially appealing today is that even as MS-65 specimens, they carry a price that is generally below $20, though the coin remains elusive and in moderately short supply.

Why is a coin like this a best buy? First, the mint made more half dollars at the New Orleans and Philadelphia Mint in 1854, than they did at the Denver Mint in 1970, or, many other years in between, making this a very low mintage coin. Originally sold to collectors, and only as part of the official mint sets, many of these coins have long since been broken out because of their low mintages, but nonetheless are available in relatively limited quantities. (From this standpoint, the 1970-D mint set itself is a bargain that ought to be included in your rare coin retirement portfolio, but the half dollar is the keystone to the project.) It is unlikely, for example, that someone would put together as many as

100,000 coins, or even as many as 20,000. But hoards into the hundreds can be found. Thus, it is a coin that could be mass-marketed, but it also has substantial appeal to collectors.

The reason that half dollars didn't circulate in 1970 is that the coin has a 40 percent silver composition. (Before you rush to calculate it, it's about .14 troy ounces of silver compared with .36 troy ounces for a regular, standard half dollar issued prior to 1965.) When the Coinage Act of 1965 was passed, silver was removed from the dime and quarter, and clad coinage was introduced for all coins with a face value of 10 cents or more. As a political compromise, a 40 percent silver half dollar was authorized to reduce the likelihood that the nominal value of the coin would exceed its face value.

In 1970, mint officials presented legislation to Congress that would remove silver from the half dollar entirely, and would authorize a new Eisenhower dollar.

The reason for this legislation was that the price of silver had been rising. It was averaging over $1.70 an ounce, and while the old 90 percent silver could be melted at $1.29 an ounce and the new silver could go to $2.90, there was consistent pressure that mint officials knew would eventually destroy all silver coinage.

The mint's original plan was to produce a 40 percent silver coin as a bonus for collectors, and then go with a copper-nickel coin for circulation once Congress authorized the new coin. The legislative process had other options.

The 1970-D Kennedy Half Dollar

Not until December 30, 1970, was the One Bank Holding Company Act passed, authorizing the Ike dollar, eliminating silver from the half dollar, and accomplishing some other numismatic housekeeping items. The result was that the silver coins that were struck for collectors ended up being the only half dollars produced that year.

For collectors of the John F. Kennedy half dollar (easily one of the world's most popular coins) the coin's date and mintmark make it a key to set completion, and because it is a last year of issue-type (in 40 percent silver), it is even more sought after.

The Gilroy Roberts portrait of John F. Kennedy and the Frank Gasparro rendering of the presidential seal on the reverse add up to an attractive coin, with an attractive price, that would make a valuable addition to your rare coin retirement portfolio.

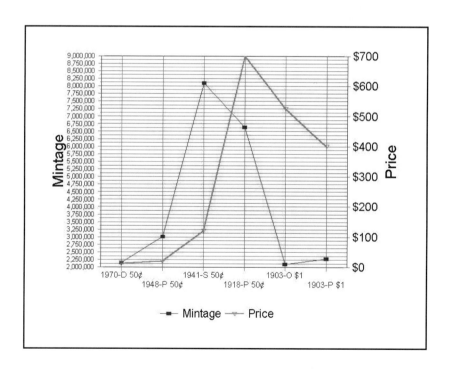

1970-S Kennedy Half Dollar
(proof) ($8)

A perennial favorite coin for a portfolio that is destined to grow is the 1970-S half dollar. It was the first of the contemporary proof coins that were struck exclusively for collectors, but was of such low mintage (2.6 million) that it is an attractive coin that should go places.

Typically collected as an individual coin, or as part of the proof set for that year, the 1970-S is a means by which you can help plan your rare coin retirement because of its low relative mintage, its essential status for completeness of a set of Kennedy halves, and low relative value that is poised for future advance.

Like its uncirculated set counterpart (the 1970-D, separately discussed in the previous chapter), the 1970-S exists because the mint seriously miscalculated the time that it would take Congress to enact legislation to eliminate silver from the half dollar, and to create an Eisenhower dollar.

The passage of the Coinage Act of 1965 had seriously undermined the long-standing good relationship that the mint had with Congress. At the time that the legislation was proposed, there was a keen focus on removal of silver from the half dollar. Sharp questions were asked at hearings before the House Banking and Currency Committee, especially by Chairman Wright Patman, D-Texas. One question in particular he asked Mint Director Eva B. Adams was why the half dollar's silver content was being retained in the first place.

Patman bought into the Treasury's argument, but it came back to haunt them when they asked for permission to remove silver entirely from the coin just four years later. Patman used the chair's prerogative to delay action for more than a year, principally because he felt that he had been lied to in 1965.

Delay followed delay, and what was to be part of the Coinage Act of 1969 slowly devolved into legislation going nowhere fast. The Nixon administration finally persuaded allies to attach the proposal to the One Bank Holding Company Act of 1970, which was dear to Chairman Patman, and the coin problem was solved.

The mint, however, had no intention of producing silver coinage for circulation: these coins had been intended strictly as a bonus for collectors. The real bonus turned out to be that there were no circulating coins made that year, so for the first time, the U.S. Mint moved into the area of non-circulating legal tender coins that served no purpose other than as collectibles. Proof coins and proof sets had been made for many years. This marked the first time, however, that the mint decided not to release counterparts of the proof date and mintmark into circulation. These coins were all produced only as a part of proof sets; the individual coins all come from sets that have been stripped of the 1970-S half dollar. Surprisingly, the 1970-S proof set sells for only about $10 (the same price, by the way, as the 1970 mint sets with the scarce 1970-D half dollar).

Proof-only issues from the mint started in 1968, but the coins that were included had other coins placed in circulation in the proof sets. (That year, Philadelphia and Denver issued half dollar coins). The 1970 was different: Philadelphia produced no circulation strikes, and neither did Denver (except for the mint sets).

Produced at the San Francisco Assay Office (later the San Francisco Mint), the 1970-S half dollar can be easily acquired so long as you don't seek quantity. For your rare coin retirement portfolio, my suggestion is that you use your resources to buy as many as a dozen of them (it should run under $100).

Like the other Kennedy half dollars produced from 1965 to 1970, this coin has .14 troy ounces of silver. When the price of silver reached $80 an ounce in 1980, the metal content of this coin was over $11, but it is likely that a substantial number of them reached the melting cauldrons. With a mintage of 2.6 million pieces, it has a lower quantity of potential availability than any Franklin half dollar (produced 1948-1963), so this is a coin with a promising future.

No one can predict the future, but consider a coin of 2.6 million mintage in superior condition from a popular series for your portfolio. This seems like one possibility where the sky's the limit, and why multiple examples belong in your rare coin retirement planner.

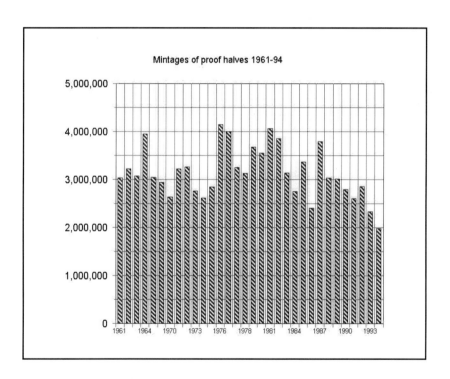

Washington Quarters
(1941-64) ($260)

First of the truly circulating commemorative coins was the Washington quarter, authorized by Congress in 1931 to commemorate the bicentennial of George Washington's birth. Intended as a one year commemoration, the party that resulted must have been grand, because more than sixty-five years later, the coin is still in circulation—a veritable workhorse in the American economy.

A generation ago, Research Triangle Institute surveyed American coinage on behalf of the U.S. Mint as it planned the future. The one coin for which no change was contemplated was the quarter, which had no attrition at all, compared with 80 percent for each 1-cent coin that was produced.

George Washington has figured in commemorative coinage in more ways than one. In 1900, the first commemorative silver dollar depicted George Washington and Marquis de Lafayette; the 1932 bicentennial marked the introduction of a circulating commemorative; and in 1982, for the 250th anniversary of his birth, Washington was honored with yet another coin greeted with delight among collectors, the first modern legal tender commemorative struck in proof and uncirculated. As you plan your rare coin retirement, the Washington quarter series as a complete collection is too expensive to include. A complete set from 1932 to the present sells for more than $2,100 in uncirculated condition. But the "short" set from 1941 to 1964 (all 90 percent silver) works quite well, and even at $260 for a current set, the price averages about $4 per coin, making it not only includible, but also a set that you almost cannot resist.

Washington Quarter Sets 1941-1964
Photo Credit: Numismatic News/Krause Publications

Back in 1979 and 1980, this was a set that actually sold for more than $800, so at today's prices, it constitutes a veritable bargain. Based on its low mintages, it also has real possibilities for substantive gain in the years ahead.

Quarters after 1953 don't have a substantial amount of value (and those after 1955 are valued at a little less than $4 a coin), but from between 1941 and 1953 are nice coins in the $10 to $15 price range, with the 1941-S (mintage 16 million) and the 1943-S (mintage 21.7 million) showing *Guidebook* prices of more than $60 apiece. Add the other war dates, such as 1944-D (14.6 million) and the 1944-S (mintage 12.5 million), and those of 1945-D (12.3 million) and 1945-S (17 million)—all of which are $20 coins or more—and you already have the value of the set without including the other coins.

If you follow an exponential analysis (see chart on page 114), the Washington quarter begins low, and ends high with a potential market price of $550.

Design for the coin is by John Flanagan, a New York sculptor, whose portrait is modeled on the bust of Washington by Houdon. It was chosen by Secretary of the Treasury Andrew Mellon over a less traditional, but aesthetically more exciting design by Lauren Gardin Fraser, (whose design was picked by the Commission on Fine Arts.)

It is thought that the 1997 congressional proposal to reinstitute circulating commemorative coinage starting in 1999, could well mark a resurgence of this long, and interesting series of coins. Certainly, given the high degree of use of the denomination, this is a strong possibility.

Switching to a series that will take ten years to complete as the congressional legal tender commemoration contemplates—will mark the close of the Washington quarter series as we presently know it. The state commemoration series will become a sub-series known and collected by itself. That has experts such as John Kamin, publisher of the *Forecaster* newsletter for the past thirty-five years, convinced that the Washington quarter series could once again make a move and capture the glory that it almost had in 1980. Of course there are those who would suggest that the sales of new series, still using the familiar Washington portrait, will suffer from malaise, and that the older series will succumb to the same fate. That would result in a moribund series with virtually no growth potential.

What seems clear enough is that for most investment planning involving rare coins, the Washington quarter set from 1941 to 1964 would be a profitable addition—one that could well rise substantially in value, and could make a substantial profit as you plan for your rare coin retirement.

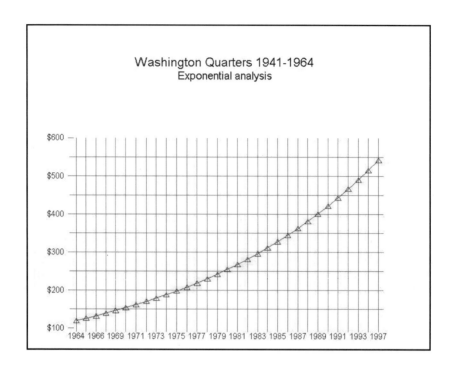

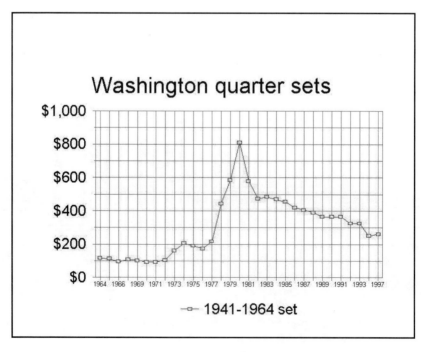

Washington Quarters
(1965-1997) ($95)

Here is an interesting series that shows an almost steadily upward progression from 1976, the first year that the *Coin Dealer Newsletter* began to carry separate price quotes for the modern Washington quarter issues, 1965 to date. A linear graph on page 117 shows a decidedly upward rate of change, sometimes as much as 10 percent each year, on a modern series that you can buy coins for from the mint, or even acquire (some) from pocket change.

Like any potential investment, the Washington quarters have ups and downs, but the graph shows that the rate of change is not all that significant. Presently, it's at a relatively low point that affords the opportunity for substantial future growth. Part of the reason for that is that the series continues to grow, even as it is threatened with its own demise—thanks to a proposed ten year program that would strike commemorative coins for all fifty states using a Washington quarter for the common obverse. That would all but put an end to the series by 1999. At that point the series would have a total of thirty-five years of coins, a nice span for most collectors. Significantly, it would also be a series with some scarce issues as well as some very common ones.

Most of the scarce issues can be defined in terms of the proof and proof only issues which have the lowest mintages. The 1968-S, for example, has a mintage of 3.0 million, while the 1969-S has a mintage of 2.9 million and the 1974-S a mere 2.6 million, not only for the proofs, but for all issues of that mintage.

The silver proof issues beginning with 1992 have possibilities as well (skip the first year of issue and go for the 1993 through coins 1996 with their much lower mintages). All have very modest mintages, and even more modest pricing.

Among the early Washington quarters, only six have mintages of under three million coins: the 1932-D, 1932-S, 1937-S, 1938-S, 1939-S and 1940-D. These coins have substantial prices today, yet the coins from the 1970s through the 1990s with lower mintages are not yet a collector's favorite. They could well be in the future, however.

John Kamin, the economist who has published *The Forecaster* newsletter since the 1960s, believes that the changeover to circulating commemorative coinage could cause a massive reevaluation of the Washington quarter series, and make the contemporary coins that are needed to complete a set surge in value. For a while, that's what happened to the series after the bicentennial quarter design was adopted in 1975-6. The price shot upward, moving at a rate of 10 percent per year. Not a bad rate of return for any investment over the long haul.

If the series does end, there's not much for these coins to do except to move up. They are so low right now as to be almost ridiculous in terms of comparison. Imagine that the 1940-D quarter with 2.78 million minted, has a selling price in uncirculated of about $40. The 1970-S proof quarter with only 2.6 million pieces minted, has a selling price of about $1.50. This is a substantial opportunity to get in on the ground floor and be there for the price rise when it does come.

Either is easy to manage and a nice way to allow you to show off your acquisition to your colleagues, friends or neighbors. It also allows you to keep them in an order that allows for quick supplementation, and counting.

Progress with a series like this can be painstaking and slow, but the growth in the decade of the nineties alone has been substantial, and that is good news for the future—one that has you planning for your rare coin retirement with coins that can show profits.

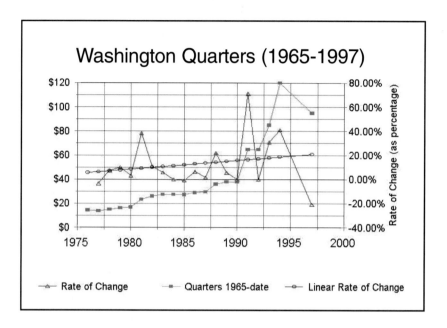

Washington Quarters (1965-1997)

1904-O Silver Dollar,
MS-65 ($95)

No story about silver dollars, nor a rare coin retirement portfolio complete, without the 1904-O Morgan silver dollar—another rarity that is almost on par with the 1903-O, and whose value history is every bit as impressive. Mint records show that 3.7 million were struck, about on par with other silver dollar issues at the turn of the century. Despite this, the coin was genuinely scarce almost from its time of striking until the early 1960s.

Initially, no one was precisely sure why, but the 1904-O was generally unavailable, hardly any were encountered in circulation, and despite what happened later, very few 1904-O dollars ever made it into circulation to become worn.

The principal cause of this is that 1904 was the last year that silver dollars were produced at the New Orleans Mint; after nearly eighty years of operating in the balmy climes of the Crescent City, the mint was on its last legs, finally ceasing its operations in 1909.

Silver dollars were stored in vaults inside the French Quarter building for about a quarter of a century. The Great Depression meant that even an old mint storage facility could be cut back, and all of the coins in the vault were shipped to an uncertain fate in Philadelphia.

By November, 1930, William Winters advertised in *The Numismatist* that he would sell the 1904-O dollar for $1.35 in uncirculated. In the same ad, proof half dimes of 1862, 1868, 1870 and 1873 were just 30¢ apiece; FCC Boyd was selling an uncirculated 1909-S VDB cent for 25¢. Wayte Raymond's first *Standard Catalogue of United States Coins* (1937) carried a $6 value for the coin;

1904-O Silver Dollar (MS-65)
Photo Credit: Numismatic News/Krause Publications

the 1909-S VDB cent was $2.50, and uncirculated twentieth-century Barber quarters were from $2.50 to $4 a coin.

By the time that the 1963 *Guide Book of United States Coins* was published (in 1962), the coin carried a $350 price tag. Again, for comparison, an uncirculated 1909-S VDB cent was $165 while common date Barber quarters were $13 in uncirculated condition.

In October, 1962, about three months after the *Red Book* was published, the bottom fell out of the market for 1904-O silver dollars. By year's end, the fledgling *Coin Dealer's Newsletter,* known as the "Grey Sheet," was listing the coins at just $1.50 apiece. The reason was the long-stored bags at the Philadelphia Mint were removed from storage and released into the stream of commerce by the hundreds of thousands. Today, there are probably more 1904-O uncirculated dollars than any other coin minted after 1885. Indeed, more than 45,000 of the coins have been certified by PCGS as MS-63, MS-64, or MS-65, the highest number of any date since 1887.

Prices tumbled to less than a tenth of their former level for reasons that were clear. Supply and demand previously found this to be a coin in demand with little supply; the supply changed, the demand remained constant, the price fell dramatically.

Flash forward a couple of years to when the market had absorbed the supply of 1904-O dollars. Minting and melting records of the United States Mint disclose that nearly half of all the silver dollars minted prior to 1904 were melted in the cauldrons of the mint following passage of the Pittman Act in 1918. While there is no census as to what was melted, or in what order, it is clear that the minting statistics for these coins are not reliable.

Up until 1958, hundreds of millions of silver dollars were found in bank vaults throughout the country. That year, coin collectors and others began to withdraw them at the rate of between 16 to 30 million coins annually such that by 1963, less than 100 million coins remained.

Even with a large quantity available, the coin's track record is a good one. Q. David Bowers, in his definitive *Encyclopedia of Silver Dollars* (1993) shows a high of $625 for an MS-65 specimen in 1986. Subsequently, the price has gone down a slope to about $95 for an MS-65 specimen. Its upside remains high, however, and in a bull market, the MS-65 and better specimens could yield substantial price increases. (Only 5,000 are certified as MS-65.) This is a coin with a bright future, and if placed in your rare coin retirement plan, could help make your future bright, too.

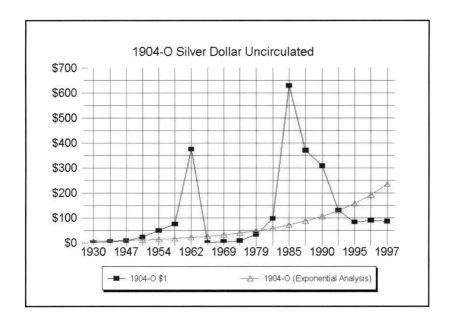

Isle of Man 1/25 Ounce Gold Crown
BU Cats 1989 (Persian) and 1996 (Burmese) ($22 each)

The Isle of Man, located in the Irish Sea about halfway between Great Britain and Ireland,is one of the oldest dependencies of the British crown.

Internal affairs on the island are ruled by a parliament (the Tynwald Court) that is more than 1,000 years old, though British laws do apply when passed by the island's own parliament and if the Isle of Man is mentioned by name.

Just 227 square miles in size (as a point of comparison, Rhode Island, America's smallest state is about 1,045 square miles in size,) the Isle of Man has about 65,000 inhabitants whose primary language is a Celtic language called Manx; English is a second language.

As you plan your rare coin retirement, the Isle of Man becomes relevant because today it is also among the most prolific coin producers in the world. Perhaps it is fitting, for in the world of stamps, as well as in coins, it is the tiniest of nations that generally offer the widest selection.

Many Isle of Man issues of 5,000 pieces or more are common, relatively speaking, and fully capable of being absorbed into the marketplace. Two recent issues, each containing 1/25 of an ounce of gold (1 crown), seem to have good potential for advancement, principally based on the popularity of the subject matter: cats.

The series started with a Manx cat—unique to the Isle of Man—in 1988, and has progressed ever since. The Persian came in 1989, and by the following year, the alley cat was added. Then came a Norwegian (1991), Siamese (1992), Main Coon (1993), Japanese Bobtail (1994), Turkish (1995), and Burmese (1996), all with maximum mintages of around 25,000 pieces. Ancillary uses for these particular coins are primarily in the jewelry field, where they have been mounted as pins, bezelled as a neck piece, or even made into a ring.

The producer of the Isle of Man coinage is the Pobjoy Mint, and it is with considerable irony that in looking at contemporary coin catalogues that list coin issues by design, date and denomination, there are more issues from this tiny island than for almost any other country.

Given that gold sells for a substantial premium over the price of a troy ounce, the ratio here (gold is at a little above $800 an ounce) is not extravagant, and fits nicely into a collecting program that includes series that can be completed. (All of the BU coins sell for about bullion value plus 20 percent at the present time). Gold's present price is around $320 an ounce, and if the price were to turn around and rise, even small coins like the 1 crown 1/25 ounce issues would benefit. There is little historic precedence for gold to remain at these price levels. Indeed, there's every reason to believe that the price will reverse and go back to historic highs—but its failure to do so could leave this as a dead asset, except as a collectible.

Here is when this coin ought to be considered for your rare coin retirement portfolio:

- You believe that the price of gold will increase above its presently abysmal rates ($320 an ounce) to the $500 or above range. That in and of itself would move the value of this coin upward.

- You are willing to invest in the series (presently 10 years duration) at about $25 a coin and keep it updated. A complete series has more appeal to some collectors and is likely to achieve a better resale price.

- You believe that cat collectors throughout the country (and perhaps the world) are a potential market for a bullion (legal tender) coin, and upon resale, you will target them to make the purchase from your rare coin retirement account.

No, there are no guarantees in life, but the relatively low mintages of Pobjoy Mint products, the thousand year history of the Isle of Man, and the nifty design on these coins all combine to make these a good investment for your portfolio.

U.S. Proof Set Collection
(1950-1997) ($1,300)

Your rare coin retirement portfolio can be looked at from several angles, one of which is the goal of having a diversified investment spread over many coins with an aggregate cost of not more than $10,000. When looked at from the standpoint of having 100 coins in the collection that average $100 per coin, this reaches the $10,000 total, but doesn't take into account variations that complete sets afford.

Collecting modern proof sets covering the years 1950-1997 is a great opportunity. With a mimimum of five coins each year, 1-cent through 50 cent pieces, proof sets offer 235 coins at a minimum. If they all sold individually, at even $10 a coin (on the average), the sets would be in the scope of your rare coin retirement plan. While you can't buy some of them individually, this is a rare opportunity to include a unique collection whose future can only be bright within the scope of your overall rare coin retirement plan.

Proof sets are specially struck coins made by the mint using highly polished planchets. They are extremely attractive, brilliant, mirror-like and widely collected. In the late twentieth century, the set consists of the cent, nickel, dime, quarter and half-dollar, though recently the Eisenhower or Anthony dollars were also included. Mintages range from the tens of thousands in the early 1950s to as many as 3.9 million in 1964 at the height of the coin collecting frenzy.

Proof set production was suspended in 1965 because of the nation's coin shortage, and when it was resumed in 1968, they were no longer packed in thin pliofilm containers, but rather in

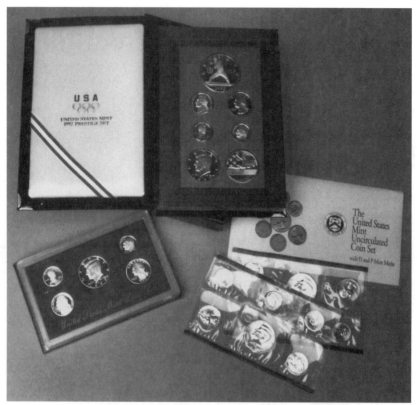

U. S. Proof Set Collection 1950-1997 (complete)
Photo Credit: Numismatic News/Krause Publications

rock-hard plastic (a type of Lucite), which forever changed the ease and facility with which the coins were removed and placed into individual collections.

Surprisingly, the 1968 and 1969 sets—with a 40 percent silver half-dollar—are still modestly priced at under $5 a piece. This is fortuitous, because it allows us to pair two sets like this with another, more expensive set from the early 1950s allowing us to obtain an average price of $100, even though the actual price differential is far more substantial. This is entirely fair because what you're really looking at is an overall collection of coins consisting of hundreds of pieces (recall the set consisted of at least five coins) rather than a single coin.

Contemporary proof coins, and indeed contemporary proof sets, have the good historic track record to fall back on, especially in the the long-term. If you find that you are bitten by the collecting bug, you may even want to go back and add some of the older modern proof sets from 1936 to 1942. While these sets are more expensive, and hence outside the scope of your rare coin retirement portfolio, they do nicely round out a collection of contemporary proof coins.

The graph on page 130 shows the mintage figures for each of the proof sets that are involved. Unlike the earlier sets from 1936 through 1942, and the old-time proof sets, proof coins were not individually available by these dates. The maximum number of proof coins is thus determined by the number of sets from 1950 to date.

For almost any advanced collector, it is desirable to have these proof coins—hence the value (particularly among the earlier items) of the sets.

The 1950 proof set (with a price of between $215 and $325) is a bit pricier than most of the coins planned for your rare coin retirement, but it averages out nicely with the later issues. And besides, with a mintage of just 51,386 sets, it's an important addition. The 1951, with a range of $190 to $265 similarly adds very low mintage of 57,500 sets to the mix.

As for the more contemporary issues, they exist in large enough quantities (but are still relatively scarce) so as to allow their marketing by telemarketers or others who might seek to obtain a substantial quantity of them, which causes the price to increase. On that basis, there is every reason to believe that these are sets with a bright future.

Not to be included in your rare coin retirement portfolio are proof sets that have errors. This includes the 1968-S set where the dime has no mintmark; the 1970-S missing the mintmark on the dime; 1971-S missing the mintmark on the nickel, 1975 missing the mintmark on the dime. These sets sell for hundreds of dollars each (mintages are very low), and you may decide to expand your rare coin retirement collection to include them, but they should not be included in your $10,000 rare coin portfolio.

Coins that should be included: the special silver proof sets that began in 1992-S, which are widely sought by collectors. The aggregate fifty-two set package is available for about $1,300—making it a bargain.

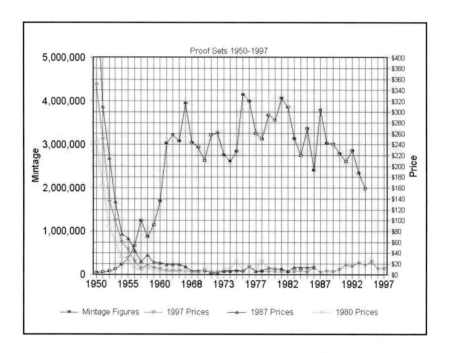

1988-W Olympic $5 Gold Coin

(BU) $99

America's journey to commemorate the Olympic Games began as a tribute, and ended up as big business for the United States Mint, which produced the coins and made a substantial profit, as well as for the U.S. Olympic Committee, which benefitted from the munificence of collectors seeking to acquire the coins.

The 1984 Olympic Games at Los Angeles were duly commemorated with two silver dollars and a gold $10 Eagle (mintmarks were later added to stimulate sales), and many thought that would be the end of it until the Games came back to the United States (which they did, in 1996, at Atlanta). Instead, lobbyists for the U.S.O.C. pushed hard to commemorate the 1988 Olympic Games at Seoul. The response was the production of a silver dollar and $5 gold piece, even though the Games themselves were more than 10,000 miles away from the United States.

Ambitious in scope, the 1988 Olympic coin program originally contemplated one million $5 gold coins and 10 million silver dollars—that would have earned the program $70 million (at $7 per silver dollar) for the small-denomination, and $35 million from the sale of the gold coin. What resulted was about $24 million in surcharges given to the Olympic committee and the first of a series of disappointments in sales to collectors, who quickly were beginning to resent being offered coins not commemorative of events held in America.

Not that the sales records were disappointing; they were disappointing only relative to the sponsor's expectations. The overall sale of 413,055 gold half Eagles ($5) was worthwhile, and the intricate, delicate head of Liberty (Nike) by Chief Engraver Elizabeth Jones, and the modernistic Olympic flame done so artfully by Marcel Jovine make this a beautiful coin to collect. From perspective of your rare coin retirement portfolio, the coin you purchase ought to be the uncirculated version (mintage just 62,913), and ought to be collected not for its beauty, but for its rarity and likelihood of future profit potential. It is unrealized potential, as of now, however. The coin originally sold for $185 in uncirculated condition, with a $35 surcharge. (In realistic parlance, that means that without the surcharge, it should have had a selling price of around $150). The price in 1997, however, has fallen to a mere $99—no doubt fueled by the decline in the price of gold.

After the pre-order period, the price went up to $225 per coin, making today's $99 price offering a bargain. (By 1990, the price had declined to a more realistic $145, and has gone down since then because of the link to the prices of precious metals).

The first of these coins was struck May 2, 1988, at the West Point Mint, formerly the Bullion Depositary, located on the military reservation of the United States Military Academy at West Point, New York. Simultaneously first strike ceremonies were held at the Denver Mint for the silver dollars also released that day.

In quiet contrast to first strike ceremonies that were previously held at West Point for the 1984 Olympic Commemorative Coin Program, and celebrations for the first strike of subsequent issues, there was no band from the Army Corps of Cadets, no expansive list of dignitaries, and no gaggle of press photographers to record the events. Instead, there was a modern telecommunications hook-up that permitted the strains of military music to be piped over a loud speaker into the minting facilities at West Point, where a crowd waited expectantly to witness the first production of commemorative coinage at the newly designated minting facility.

What makes this particular coin attractive as part of your investment portfolio is its relatively modest mintage, which compares nicely with many other gold coins, for example, the 1904-S $5 gold piece (mintage 97,000) or the 1893-CC (mintage 60,000), which both have a substantially higher value than their Olympic counterpart.

Although the coin marks the beginning of the abuse of the commemorative coinage system in modern times, the uncirculated example is likely to become a key in future sets that include contemporary gold coins, Olympic coins and perhaps other assembled displays.

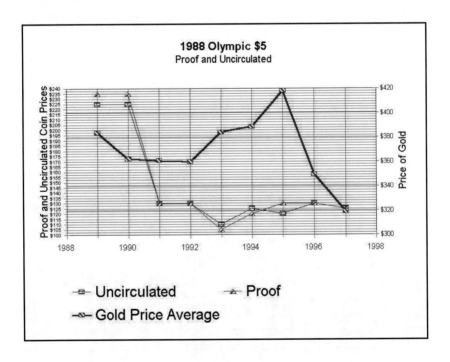

Gem Proof Silver Eagles
1986-1996 ($300 set of 12)

America entered the international area of a silver bullion coin rather late in the game, in 1986, but it quickly became a world leader with more than 62 million uncirculated pieces sold, each representing one troy ounce of silver.

You can purchase a complete set of twelve coins for under $90 at the present time, but with the mintages averaging between three and five million pieces, this seems unlikely to be a good investment value in the foreseeable future. Concentrate instead on, or at least consider, the proof bullion coins issued and struck at the San Francisco Mint from 1986 to the present. You might also include a special 1995 "W" mint struck at West Point Mint to commemorate the tenth anniversary of the eagle; only 30,000 were minted, and the aftermarket for this coin is now around $700 apiece. It's not included in your rare coin portfolio for that reason, though if you included it, you could easily average the cost out to $100 per coin, and this is probably not a bad option to consider.

The first year of issue, 1986, had a high mintage of 1.4 million pieces; by the second year, the mintage had declined to 904,732 pieces, and the third year to 557,000. For the next several years, that was the range of production—about where production of U.S. proof sets were in 1956.

It continued to dip in 1993 and 1994 as mintages went to 403,000 and 372,000, respectively. And at those levels, you have to start comparing them to some of the more scarce Carson City silver dollars that, even in hoard quantities, have increased in value through the years.

Silver Eagle Sets 1986-1996 (Gem Proof)
Photo Credit: Numismatic News/Krause Publications

The force behind the bullion program for both gold and silver was fear: fear of inflation, fear of renewed recession, fear of heightened unemployment, fear that the economy was about to stall once again, and fear of a host of other possibilities. In reality, it was fear of the unknown that fueled the marketplace, as investors, bit players in the precious metals market, and many others, eagerly attempted to cash in on marketplace movement.

"It doesn't matter whether the market goes up, or down, just as long as it's not stagnant," said Burton S. Blumert, of Camino Coin Burlingame, California, an acknowledged expert in the precious metals field. Adds James DiGeorgia, editor of the *Gold and Silver Report,* the real message is, "it's about the economy."

Silver has not been immune to these changes. Even after the Coinage Act of 1873 demonetized silver, and prevented its "free coinage" from bullion into money, its price reacted to events in the marketplace. To be sure, after the Coinage Act, and with the rapid mining of the Comstock Lode in Nevada, the price of silver initially fell, and continued to do so for nearly fifty years. However, in the immediate post-World War I era, when India put impressive demands on silver, the price of silver rose again to the point at which it was profitable to melt existing silver coinage for its precious metal content.

In the marketplace, American silver coins minted prior to 1965 were often offered in $1,000 face value bags—a means by which it would be possible to own bullion and coinage at the same time. Foreign nations stepped into the breach, and the Mexican onza was the first real attempt to tap into the silver market.

Of course what happened to precious metals in 1979-80 also had a great deal to do with the interest in silver; an attempt was made to corner the silver market, similar to what Jay Gould tried to do with the gold market during the American Civil War. This one was attempted by the Hunt Brothers, Texas billionaires, who slowly started to acquire bullion stocks until they had most of the available stockpile under their control. The price rose, until it topped $48 an ounce, and was poised to go still higher. With warehouse metal unavailable, silver coins flooded into the market for melting—together with George III tea services, and other similar antiques.

The collapse of the effort to corner the marketplace left silver in a deep hole, but it emerged and with it came this delightful bullion coin with a proof version specifically produced for collectors.

Rarities right now include the 1988-S (557,000 pieces minted and a $36 coin), the 1993-S (403,000 pieces minted and a $45 coin), the 1994 (372,000 pieces minted, a $40 coin), and the 1995 and 1996, whose mintage figures have been slow to come from Washington, but which trade on presumed low mintages between $25 and $40 apiece.

In the future, this coin set may show more promise, especially when compared to some comparable silver dollar issues. Low mintage, large coin size, and marketability are its keys to a bright future in your rare coin retirement.

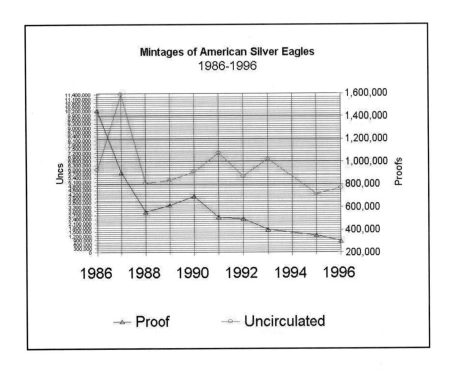

1991 Quarter Ounce $10 Gold American Eagle
(Uncirculated)

Gold and gold coinage have had a long and fascinating history in America. The earliest of the minting and coinage laws of 1792 call for gold, silver and copper coinage. Gold coinage is even mentioned in the Constitution in one of the powers of Congress enumerated in Article I, section 8. On that basis alone, you need to consider it as you plan your rare coin retirement.

Gold coinage was recalled during the administration of Franklin D. Roosevelt, and for the succeeding half century, the mere mention of a gold commemorative coin or any private ownership of gold was enough to cause Treasury Department apoplexy.

This all ended in December, 1974, when Americans regained the right to own gold, even though the only contemporary gold coins that could be acquired were South African krugerrands, and later the Canadian Maple Leaf.

America's rush into the gold bullion market started with the gold Eagles of 1986, using a familiar rendering of the obverse of the double Eagle designed by Augustus Saint-Gaudens at the turn of the century, which was joined with a family of Eagles initially sculpted by Miley Busiek of Dallas, Texas.

Starting with a one ounce gold coin (with a $50 face value), and including a half ounce ($25 face value), a quarter ounce ($10 face value) and a tenth of an ounce ($5 face value) coins, the series was billed as an answer to foreign competition—the

American krugerrand. It soon knocked its competition out of the box, with over 1.3 million one ounce coins issued in the first year alone. But that was the focus of the attention. The lesser denominations had substantially lower mintages.

Plans for your rare coin retirement should include gold coinage; yes, it's possible to have gold included, and even to get rare coins that should appreciate nicely in price in the coming dozen years.

A "best buy" can be inexpensive in overall price, or just relatively speaking. If the list price of a Cadillac is $34,000, then it is a "best buy" at $20,000, even though a Chevrolet may cost a lot less, and do more or less the same thing.

When Walter Pershke paid $410,000 for the first Brasher doubloon sold in more than 60 years (the Friedberg Family specimen sold at the RARCOA section of Auction '79) it didn't appear to be a best buy, but rather an expensive acquisition. It became a "best buy" not too long later when the Garrett Collection was sold by Bowers & Ruddy Galleries, and another Brasher doubloon—of equal mystique and condition—brought a price several hundred thousand dollars higher: $725,000 was paid by a private collector from Long Island, New York. When a collector pays the mint $5 for a proof set, and the mint delivers a set with the "S" mintmark missing from the nickel (as it did about 1,700 times in 1971), that is a best buy, because, the set has a value of more than $1,200 today.

Best buys, then, can be expensive, or inexpensive. What counts is relative price. Compared to something else in the marketplace, a numismatic item carries a weight all its own, and can be a bargain because of this, even if not an immediately recognizable one.

What they really are can best be described as a "cherry picked" item, something that the buyer knows more about than the seller. And it is for that reason that knowledge about numismatic purchases takes on considerable importance, and the motto "Buy the book before the coin" offers indisputably valuable advice.

One best buy that you should consider for your rare coin

retirement is the 1991 quarter ounce $10 gold bullion piece (mintage 36,100). It is a scarce coin whose metal content still largely determines its value. (With gold at its current price, that means the coin has about $80 worth of precious metal in it.) Recent selling prices for the coin average $99 to $107. Mintage for the coin is relatively modest. A similar coin, also about a quarter of an ounce of gold, is the $5 gold piece. To get a mintage that low, you have to travel back to the very rare 1909-O (mintage 34,200); before that, it's the 1894-O (16,600 mintage).

Because its gold content is modest, and the premium for the uncirculated so minimal, there is virtually no downside—unless the price of gold declines precipitously. The upside is that once collectors see that this is a series to collect, it could just go out of sight.

$5 Gold Piece
Liberty Type (1866-1908)
BU ($144)
Selected dates: 1899, 1900,
1901-S, 1902-S, 1903,
1903-S, 1904,
1906, 1906-D, 1907,
1907-D, 1908

These are coins that have a lot going for them, even if they do cost a little bit more than the $100 average that we're using. But since there are some other coins that cost a lot less, this is the easiest way to effectively add to your rare coin retirement while at the same time getting substantial value for your money.

Here are a dozen United States Mint issued half Eagles—a gold piece with a face value of $5, and a gold content equal to .24186 troy ounces of fine gold, all minted as .900 fine. Each, would make a fine addition to your rare coin retirement.

These gold half Eagles:

- Have their nominal face value of $5 per coin

- Have their bullion value equal to about a quarter of an ounce of gold. At $320 an ounce, the coin has about $80 worth of gold content. The remaining $60 is pure numismatic content, not a bad deal under any circumstances.

- Relative mintage of these coins is small, ranging from 227,000 for the 1903 to a little over one million coins for some of the others.

- Virtually all of these coins had their mintages reduced by the great government gold coin melts of the 1930s through 1950s.

- The number of surviving coins in uncirculated condition is a relatively small percentage of the overall mintage.

- Demand is historically high for all American gold coinage among collectors.

For hundreds of years, gold and silver have each reacted to price variations in other areas of the economy. Even when gold and silver were more formally tied to monetary value, the value of the metal—and the coin—changed from time to time, depending on not only economic conditions, but also on the politics of the day.

During the Civil War period, tycoon Jay Gould attempted to corner the gold market. For a while, he was successful, and reaped profits. Even though the price of gold had been fixed at $20.67 an ounce by the Coinage Act of 1837, the price doubled, tripled and then continued to rise as the federal government nearly bankrupted itself during the Civil War. Gold had value even if the greenbacks issued by the government did not. At one point, the government had only enough cash on hand to meet two or three days' obligations. That no doubt contributed to the rapid rise of the price of gold.

In 1932, the year that Roosevelt ran against Herbert Hoover for the presidency, America was in dire economic straits. It was four years after the American economy sneezed, and the world caught pneumonia, it was the Great Depression.

From an average gross weekly wage in the manufacturing sector of $24.76 in the 1929 it had fallen to $16.89 by 1932. In the robust economy of 1929, people averaged a forty-four hour work week; by 1932, those who could work averaged only thirty-eight hours a week, (wage earnings per hour declined from 56 cents to 44.1 cents). More than 31 million Americans were employed in 1929; by 1932, it had bottomed out to 23.6 million. Personal savings, which amounted to more than $4.2 billion in 1929, had fallen to a negative number by 1932. Indeed, total personal income had fallen from $85.9 billion in 1929 to a mere $50.2 billion in 1932—a decline of more than 40 percent. Taxes received by the government were off by a comparable amount. Drastic, economy-wide measures were required to save the country from collapse.

Those who owned gold would be immune to the desperate steps that the government was about to take, so a decision was made to make all equally susceptible to the government's cure. FDR's presidential papers offer a partial explanation as to why he nationalized gold, ended the striking of gold coins, and prohibited domestic ownership of gold bullion by most Americans. On January 31, 1934, his papers show that he wrote he was taking his action "to maintain a reasonably stable cost of living . . . to foster steadily increasing employment . . . to maintain such position of the dollar with reference to other currencies as would encourage an increasing domestic and foreign trade . . . to eliminate broad fluctuations in exchange rates without sacrificing sovereignty over our monetary policy . . . (and) to avoid competitive depreciation of currencies."

Long before FDR signed the Gold Reserve Act of 1934, he had aimed at ending all gold coinage in the country and nationalizing all gold holdings. Signing the act was merely symbolic; most Americans had been restricted in their ownership of gold coinage and bullion on a systematic basis since Roosevelt had taken office on March 4, 1933.

When Roosevelt took office, the 100 days of revitalizing the American economy began. The drive to end the private ownership of gold and the striking of gold coins began on March 6, 1933, just two days after FDR had braved the bitter snow in Washington to delivery his first inaugural address.

Telling hopeful but desolate Americans that he offered them a "New Deal," FDR could only promise "The only thing we have to fear is fear itself."

Although his aim was possibly accounted for in the explanation he gave in January 1934, it is more likely that he had an ulterior motive: to remove from the hands of the citizenry the one weapon with which any American could have wrecked the economic policies upon which the New Deal was to be based. The policy was inflation; the weapon was the restriction of ownership of gold, without which successful implementation of the inflationary monetary policy could have been prevented. This was a nation that had reached a critical choice: to implode, or to go to war and fight the Depression in a unique way—by having the government inflate the economy and spend money that it really didn't have.

On March 6, 1933, Roosevelt declared a "Bank Holiday" by invoking an obscure section of the 1917 Trading with the Enemy Act. The act permitted the president to prohibit "under such rules and regulations as he may prescribe . . . any transactions in . . . export or earmarkings of gold or silver coin or bullion . . . by any person within the United States." So Roosevelt closed the nation's banks by declaring that "there have been heavy and unwarranted withdrawals of gold and currency from our banking institutions for the purpose of hoarding; and . . . these conditions have created a national emergency."

During the banking holiday, Roosevelt prohibited the operation of any banking institution, prohibited any bank from paying out, exporting or earmarking gold or gold coins, and temporarily suspended the striking of gold coin by the mint.

Roosevelt's action was one a leading constitutional scholar wrote in 1973 was probably illegal at best, and unconstitutional at worst. Yet, the American people were desperate; a depression

$5 Gold Pieces (One Dozen Half Eagles)
Photo Credit: Numismatic News/Krause Publications

gripped the land. Roosevelt, they believed, offered salvation—a New Deal, even if it was without gold.

On March 9, 1933, the very day that the special session of Congress convened, Roosevelt submitted "The Emergency Banking Act" to them for consideration. He also sent them a message, stating that "On March 3 banking operations in the United States ceased . . . Our first task is to reopen sound banks." He called for prompt action on his legislation, for "with action taken thereon, we can proceed to the consideration of a rounded program of national restoration." A practical effect of these actions was to make each $20 gold piece worth $33.86, and each $5 coin worth a fractional proportion.

Numismatists, of course, were able to keep "rare and unusual coins," however, those who were not so lucky as to own such coins turned them in to be melted. The net result of this unique experiment was that *billions* of dollars (at today's prices) worth of rare gold coins were melted by the government as the accompanying chart summarizes:

Type	Face Value**	Total Minted 1795–1933	Total Melted 1933–1954*	Percentage Melted
$20	$3,482.1	174.105	66.47	38.2%
$10	$ 576.83	57.683	17.737	30.7%
$5	$ 394.56	78.911	16.4236	20.8%
$2.5	$ 51.07	20.426	2.4452	12%

*Millions of Pieces   **Millions of dollars (face value)

For that very reason, the mintage figures for gold coins are not an accurate indication of the number of coins in existence. The government melted at least 20 percent of them—and perhaps even more disappeared. The result is that these are truly scarce coins with real possibilities for future growth in your rare coin retirement portfolio.

When it comes to even common dates like 1899, 1900, 1901-S, 1902-S, 1903, 1903-S, 1904, 1906, 1906-D, 1907, 1907-D, and 1908, PCGS has certified only thousands of gold coins, not hundreds of thousands. For 1907, for example, about 3,000 coins have been certified or graded compared with over 626,000 struck, and a probable loss through melting of at least 120,000 coins.

These will be rare and exciting coins for your rare coin retirement portfolio, and with them included, it should grow and prosper.

Susan B. Anthony Dollar Set
(1979–1981) ($135)
and 1981 P, D, S Uncirculated $1 rolls
($55 each)

It was a coin that society was not yet ready for. A generation later, there is a significant clamor for the dollar coin denomination, as well as for its smaller size, but in 1977, as legislation that created the Susan B. Anthony dollar slugged its way across Capitol Hill, it was simply a denomination and a design ahead of its time.

Conceived based upon an efficiency expert's study, Research Triangle Institute made a 1975 recommendation that the denomination be reconstituted and shrunk in size to 26mm from the old 38.1mm size. Mint Chief Engraver Frank Gasparro went to work while the law was being debated and created an exquisite flowing hair Liberty model with a flying eagle reverse. Politics got in the way, feminists needed assuaging and in short order, a congressional staffer suggested Susan B. Anthony for instant memorialization, which is precisely what occurred.

In retrospect, the failure of the Susan B. Anthony dollar had much more to do with its lack of promotion in vending machines and its inconvenience than anything else. Arguments were raised at the time that the coin was too similar in size to the quarter (2mm less in diameter), but there are few who have confused a $1 bill with a $10 note, even though both are the same size and weight.

From the standpoint of your rare coin retirement planning, the Anthony dollar is a good addition to the portfolio. It actually gives

149

1979 Susan B. Anthony Dollar

you a complete collection with very few coins, since the Anthony dollar is among the shortest series ever produced by the U.S. Mint.

The irony is that the uncirculated coins were in such poor demand at the time of issue that they lay in Treasury Department vaults for almost two decades. Had circumstances been different, a century from now there could very have been the "great Anthony dollar sale" just as there was a "Carson City silver dollars" sale the Treasury Department the 1970s.

There are only three years of Anthony dollars to consider, 1979, 1980 and 1981, yet there are two key dates and some other possibilities. The proof-only issues actually hold the key to the issue, and three uncirculated coins are plainly a bargain that ought to be considered for the long-term.

For the uncirculated coins, consider the 1981 P, D and S coins, available and issued only in mint sets. There are 3 million of the Philadelphia Mint version, 3.25 million of the Denver Mint product, and 3.49 million from San Francisco. Compare those mintages to Morgan dollars or Peace dollars and it has the makings of a winner in future years. Besides, there is almost no downside risk. The face value is $20, and at $55 a roll, $1.50 per coin, that's one of the surest winning possibilities of all.

Other options are the 1979-S clear "S" variety (type 2), which currently sells for around $50, and the 1981-S clear "S" is a $70 coin. Either coin is a good investment possibility because of its rarity. The 1981-S variety wasn't given widespread credence as a collectible until 1994, when it finally was included in the *Red Book*. The reason for the late inclusion (the coin was not included in the 1993 massive *Bowers Encyclopedia*) is that the coin was simply deemed too common to merit extensive review. This opinion has changed, however.

There are some guesses that as many as 300,000 of these "open" or clear mintmark exist; no one will ever know for sure. But regardless, it could be an exciting addition to your rare coin retirement portfolio.

In its later years, the Susan B. Anthony dollar's reserves in the mint have been parcelled out, such that by the end of the century, they will all be dissipated, and Congress will be given a choice as to whether or not to authorize a new dollar coin, start striking the Anthony anew, or give up on the denomination as a coin entirely.

Regardless, the choice will breathe new life into this series, and in the process, could well give your rare coin retirement a significant boost.

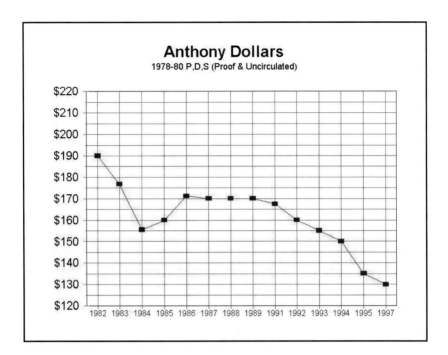

Vietnam War Memorial
Commemorative Dollar
(Uncirculated, $27)

A generation after the first war lost by the U.S. on the battlefield and on the television screen in American living rooms
ended, the nation was ready to start to view Vietnam as history,
and to attempt to suitably honor those who served.

More than 3.5 million American men and women served
in Vietnam in an involvement that began in 1957 and ended in
1973. It was the longest war in American history. More than two
million people, many of them civilians, were killed, three million
others wounded, and some 587 Americans were held as prisoners of war. Most significantly, a total of 57,685 Americans were
killed.

Depending on when they served in Vietnam, veterans are
entitled to wear up to three medals, two of which were issued by
the United States: the Armed Forces Expeditionary Service Medal
for those serving from July 1, 1958 to July 3, 1965, and the Vietnam Service Medal, for service through and including March 28,
1973, the day before the lowering of the American flag and the
U.S. Military Assistance Command Flag at Camp Alpha. The third
medal was the Republic of Vietnam's Campaign Medal, available
to recipients of the U.S.-issued Vietnam Service Medal, given to
those who served six months in direct support of military operations in Vietnam or an adjacent country. The Department of Defense specifically authorized U.S. servicemen to accept such
awards. Besides the medals, any member of the armed forces who

Vietnam War Commemorative Dollar

served in one of seventeen campaigns that constituted the war, is entitled to wear a bronze star on the service ribbon.

These medals would come to play a critical part in ultimately commemorating the Vietnam War on our national coinage more than a quarter century after the last of them was issued to a veteran or serviceman. The medals all appear on the reverse of the coin.

What is left, as the Vietnam conflict moves from current events into history, is the start of an official perspective on the conflict, in the form of the first commemorative coin issued by a nation for a war that it lost.

Commemoration of the Vietnam conflict on national coinage began with a call for issuance of a Vietnam Veterans Memorial commemorative coin bearing a design that was to be emblematic of the Vietnam Veterans Memorial in Washington.

This initially controversial national monument, located in Washington on the Mall between the Washington Monument and the Lincoln Memorial, was formally dedicated in November, 1982. Constructed entirely with private funds, it was completed two years later when President Ronald Reagan accepted the tribute in the name of the American people, and transferred the memorial to the U.S. Park Service.

No one who has visited the site is likely to forget it, or the starkness of the setting. Unlike many other buildings in Washington that have a Greek or Roman tradition in design, the Vietnam War is memorialized with two identical 250 foot, walls of polished black granite, sloping to the ground from a central apex that is ten feet tall. The name of each American serviceman and woman who died is inscribed in the Wall that was designed by a Yale architecture student, Maya Ying Lin, in a competition that featured the works of over 1,400 other artists.

Silence is the abiding sound that can be heard at the Wall as relatives look for the name of a lost loved one, and friends try and recall how meaningless the conflict was that took a young fellow countryman to the pale beyond life. Occasionally, there is a flower placed at the slabs; one day when I visited in 1993 there was a wreath of flowers, and sadly, a well-worn teddy bear.

Issued at $27 in uncirculated (including a $10 surcharge), its low mintage is just one reason why this coin belongs in a rare coin retirement portfolio. Where many other commemorative issues of modern times have declined precipitously, this one has legs and is holding its value.

You could put four uncirculated specimens into your rare coin retirement plan for just $108—and then watch in succeeding years as a future generation of collectors tries to complete their sets, and seeks out your coin.

1995 Double Die Lincoln Cent
(MS-65) $25

Minting began some 2,500 years ago, and more Lincoln Memorial cents have been produced since 1959 than any other coin in the history of coinage. That doesn't seem like a series that belongs in your rare coin retirement portfolio, but several of the coins, the latest of which was produced in 1995, form an essential part of the complete series and are vital to the completion of the set of one cent pieces.

The error in question is a doubling of the lettering, and image, on the obverse of the coin. There are other similar errors among Lincoln cents, starting with the 1955 double die cent; others include 1972 (XF at about $140), 1983 (AU at about $125), 1984 (AU at about $90). The 1995 (at about $25) is just the latest coin with this error that, when caught at the mint, is usually melted and destroyed.

Production of coins is an interesting process, and things are not quite what they appear. The "doubling" is not the result of the coin being struck twice, but rather of the die that strikes the coins having a doubled image on it. Each strike on the planchet of a coin gives the impression of a double-struck coin.

Until 1996 manufacture of coin dies was the exclusive province of the Philadelphia Mint. (In 1996, the mint opened a second die shop in Denver to split the responsibilities between two secure establishments.) The die shop operated two shifts seven days a week, 365 days a year, to fulfill the nation's coinage needs. More than 144,000 dies were produced each year at the Philadelphia Mint until 1996. That amounts to 394 dies per day,

1995 Double Die Lincoln Cent (MS-65)
Photo Credit: Numismatic News/Krause Publications

twenty-four dies per hour, or one die every two minutes. In that time, the steel has to be cut, the image plated onto it, and the die inspected. It's not hard to imagine the errors that can take place under that time pressure.

Inspectors of the process typically are middle-aged men who wear bi-focal glasses, and use magnifiers to check the intricate die work for the exactitude required. With tired eyes it is easy to make a minor mistake and miss a slight doubling of the image on the die that is going to make a coin.

That error turns out to be a collector's delight because typically it is but a single die that causes the image to be reproduced. If the error is caught by mint employees before the die does all of its work (a typical cent die has a life span of between 500,000 and 750,000 coins, or less than a day at a three-shift mint operation), it is inevitably pulled and the coins destroyed.

Once the error is bagged and enters commerce, it becomes fair game for collectors and the race is on to guess the total mintage of the error. For the 1995 double die, it is apparent that more than one die was involved, and that the degree of doubling varied. That is not a surprise given the method of production. The master hub is pressed against the metal shaft that will become the die, and impressed. The die is filled with metal that pressure forces upward and outward. There is an intense manual operation associated with lining up the hub with the die-to-be; it is evident that there was a slight miscalibration, resulting in the 1995 overdate and the appearance of doubling on the date, Liberty and the motto "In God We Trust."

From research done by several Philadelphia area dealers, it is apparent that the 1995 double die was manufactured over several days in February, 1995 (that's the first clue that more than one die was involved). Since cent production is a high speed operation—600 coins per minute, 35,000 to 36,000 coins per hour—substantial quantities of the error move quickly into the stream of commerce.

There are differing versions and examples of this mint error. For your rare coin retirement planning, seek out a better strike where the doubling is strong, and go for the best condition obtainable. A 1972 double die in AU-50 (available at around $130) would be a nice addition for a bit more money. Whichever coins you choose to purchase, the rarity of these double die cents makes them an important and potentially valuable addition to your portfolio.

Uncirculated Barber Dime
(1892-1916) MS-63 ($100)

Charles Barber served as chief engraver of the United States from 1880 until his death in 1917. No single designer or engraver of the United States Mint has influenced contemporary coin collecting more than this man. He also had a significant impact on contemporary American artistic and sculptural designs.

Charles Edward Barber was a prolific artist. His governmental career spanned twelve presidential administrations, starting in 1869 as an engraver's assistant (to his father, William, then chief engraver) when Andrew Johnson was president, and ending during as the chief engraver in the second term of Woodrow Wilson.

During that time frame, most of which (from 1880 to 1917) he spent as chief engraver, Charles Barber probably designed and

Barber Dime

Barber Dime (MS-63)
Photo Credit: Numismatic News/Krause Publications

engraved more coins and medals than any other person in the employ of the United States or any other mint, before or since.

It is a rare tribute that the work of a sculptor or engraver of coinage has his work stand the test of time; but in Barber's case, nearly seventy years after he died, his coinage designs were still being produced. (The Cuban 2-centavos coin bearing his design was still in production as late as 1985.)

The crowning achievement of this giant of sculpture and engraving came in 1892 when the design of the dime, quarter and half-dollar were simultaneously changed from the Seated Liberty design that had been used in one form or another since 1837, to the more modernistic and mature allegorical Liberty designed by Barber.

All three of these coins were workhorses of the domestic coinage scene, though widespread circulation and continued commercial usage has had the delightful effect of reducing the population of fully uncirculated coins of these issues.

As of late 1997, only about 4,000 Barber dimes of all dates and mint marks have been certified by PCGS and NGC as MS-63. There are more MS-64 Barber dimes, but fewer MS-65s, meaning that the total population of better quality uncirculated coins is limited to 10,000 or fewer.

For your rare coin retirement portfolio, an excellent choice for inclusion is the uncirculated (MS-63, choice uncirculated) Barber dime, and there are several that meet the general guideline of being priced at $100 or less. At MS-63, and priced at about $100, here are some twenty different dates and mint marks that are qualified for inclusion in your rare coin retirement portfolio. These include more than a dozen from the Philadelphia Mint alone, produced in 1902 through 1916.

From the Denver Mint, the 1908, 1911 and 1912 are good candidates. From San Francisco, the mintages are all lower, but the 1911-S, at just a bit over $100, is not a bad choice; neither is the 1916-S, which usually fits the price parameter of your rare coin retirement portfolio.

Barber's lifetime of achievement is memorialized by more than the coinage that bears his name: the Barber dime, Barber quarter and Barber half dollar, all struck starting in 1892. He also designed the less well-known Barber nickel (known in numismatic circles as the Liberty head nickel, struck from 1883 to 1913), the 1913 example of which has a value today of more than $1.5 million.

In addition to the coins that bear his name, Barber designed the Hawaiian coinage of 1883 (dime, quarter, half dollar and dollar), and at least seven commemorative coins. These include, the first commemorative, the obverse of the Columbian Exposition of 1892-3, the Isabella Quarter of 1893, the Lafayette dollar of 1900, the Louisiana Gold Purchase dollar of 1903, the Lewis & Clark exposition gold dollar of 1904, the Panama-Pacific Exposition quarter eagle and 50-cent piece of 1915, and the McKinley Memorial gold dollar of 1916. He is also credited with dozens of medals, including twenty-eight for the Annual Assay Commission alone; more than any other artist.

There is significant upside potential to these coins since, in 1979, run-of-the-mill (MS-60) uncirculated Barber dimes were selling for $120 apiece, and by 1980, the MS-60 examples from the Philadelphia Mint were bid at $250 per coin with ask about 10 percent higher.

Prices for these coins have fallen in recent years, which gives you a great opportunity to purchase these special coins at bargain prices. These coins have great potential to rise in price and to become a valuable part of your retirement portfolio.

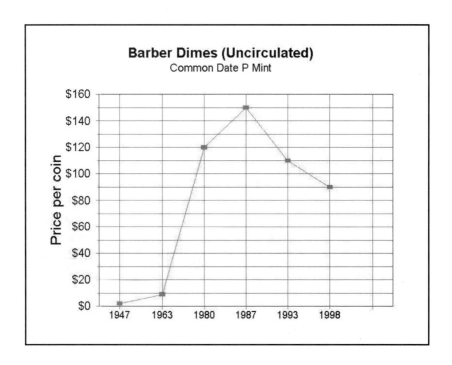

Classic U.S. Commemorative Coins

Commemorative coinage introduced primarily for collectors and as memorabilia, rather than as circulating coinage, is more than a century old in the United States. The custom of commemorative coins among the world's nations is even older, though it is only in modern times that the coinage has not been intended to circulate.

America's commemorative coinage history can be divided into two neat time frames: from 1892 to 1954, and from 1982 to the present. Since 1982, when the modern era of U.S. commemoratives began, more than 53 million coins have been struck by the U.S. Mints at Philadelphia, Denver, San Francisco and West Point, compared to just 17.6 million commemoratives struck at these mints during the golden commemorative era, 1892 to 1954.

Of these 17 million pieces that were minted, some 47 percent were melted afterwards, making a surviving total mintage for all U.S. commemoratives struck from 1892 to 1952 a low 9.4 million. By contrast, the coins for a single issue commemorating the centennial of the Statute of Liberty sold more coins than in the entire earlier period: 7.7 million of the 50-cent piece were sold, 7.1 million of the dollar, and 500,000 of the $5 gold piece.

From 1892 to 1954, there were a total of about sixty different designs authorized by Congress for commemorative purposes. This includes forty-eight different half dollar designs approved by Congress, one quarter, and one silver dollar commemorative coin. There were also ten gold coin designs produced from 1903 to 1926. Between 1982 and 1995, the mint has produced forty-seven different coins. By 1996, the number had swelled to over sixty-five different coins.

The early commemorative issues (prior to 1954) had the same problem then as they do today: oversupply. Many issues were overproduced and millions of coins melted. Resales were simply not very strong.

The 1951 Booker T. Washington half dollar set (three coins) was issued in 1951 at $8.50, and the price was raised in the Autumn of 1951 to $10 a set. In September, 1955, an ad for Ben's Stamp & Coins, Chicago, in *The Numismatist,* monthly journal of the American Numismatic Association offered to sell the set at $9. It was sold in an ad, by the way, entitled "Scarcer U.S. Coins."

Coinage from the earlier period was subject to substantial abuse. Mintages were very high and sponsors—private groups, many of whose only purpose was to profit from the commemorative coin issue—often requested that coins of identical design be issued in succeeding years. The resulting products often had low mintages, and are very rare today, but they were perceived, by at least some collectors, as the fodder for substantial abuse.

Here's a listing of at least a dozen older commemorative coins that fit into the scope of your rare coin retirement portfolio. All are priced in the $100 range in superior mint states of preservation. The grade noted is for (P) Professional Coin Grading Service, or (N) Numismatic Guaranty Corporation.

Prices for these half dollars are taken from advertisements run during the summer of 1997.

- Lincoln, MS-64(N) $125
- Maryland, MS-64(N), $110
- Rhode Island, MS-65(P), $130
- New York, MS-65(P), $127
- Iowa, MS-66(P), $100
- Arkansas 1936 MS-65(P), $127
- Washington Carver set MS-64(P) (1951 P, D, S), $110
- Booker T. Washington, 1947 MS-65(N), $80
- 1920 Pilgrim, MS-63(P), $79

- 1925 California MS-61(ANACS), $120
- Bay Bridge MS-64(P), $125
- Daniel Boone 1936-D, MS-65(P), $125
- Robinson, MS-64(N), $85

Early issues were the subject of considerable abuse by the sponsors, who (it seemed) had the mint jumping through hoops. All this changed with the issuance of the Cochran Report, which was prepared by Harry X. Boosell and issued by the chairman of the House Banking Committee in 1939. The Cochran Report recommended that commemorative coins be issued once with a single year and denomination, and recommended strongly against abusive marketing practices. It also contained a detailed examination of the real abuses of the mint's practices a half century ago when commemorative coins were struck to order, in very limited quantities. (The Oregon Trail commemorative, first issued in 1926, then again in 1928, 1933, 1934, 1936, 1938 and 1939 typifies some of the problems.) Coupled with the mint opposition to commemoratives that first surfaced in 1929, this set the stage for the 1954 cessation of commemorative issues that lasted a generation.

Commemorative coinage can be divided into three major parts: the 144 coin silver set, consisting of a single quarter (the 1893 Isabella) and dollar (the 1900 Lafayette), 142 silver half dollars (struck from 1892 to 1954); the eleven-coin gold set struck from the turn of the century until 1926; and the modern era set, starting in 1982.

Early commemorative coins can be fun to collect, and to invest in, but most are well outside the scope for use in planning your rare coin retirement because of their price when they are in superior condition. The Hawaiian 50-cent commemorative, for example, in MS-63 condition was recently being sold for $1,300, a bit pricey when your goal is 100 coins for $10,000, no matter how you do your price averaging. But there are at least a dozen commemorative coins that work into such a program—spreading across a half century of issuance with unusual designs, and themes and relatively low mintages: the elements that we look for when searching for good investment for your rare coin retirement.

Classic U.S. Commemorative Coinage
Photo Credit: Numismatic News/Krause Publications

That these coins can have enhanced value can easily be seen with one that isn't included because of its price, the Missouri Centennial half dollar of 1921 with a 2★4 punched into the field to denote the twenty-fourth state to enter the union. In *The Numismatist* of April, 1922, the Sedalia Trust Company of Sedalia, Missouri, took out a full page advertisement to promote its sale of the coin. "Specially coined to commemorate the 100th anniversary of Missouri's Admission to the Union of States," it goes on to declare that the coin is "a beautiful silver souvenir that will be highly prized by the tens of thousands of ex-Missourians scattered throughout the world, also by coin collectors." Only 5,000 of the 2★4 design were produced, sold by the Sedalia Trust Company for $1 apiece. By the summer of 1997, Heritage Galleries, of Dallas, Texas, offered a lightly toned example in MS-65 (certified by PCGS) for $4,500.

As the chart on page 170 shows, commemorative coins have had ups and downs in recent times, and they are presently at all-time lows. They can only go up from here. Obviously, not every old commemorative has that type of return, but it is possible, and that is one way for your rare coin retirement to become a valuable one.

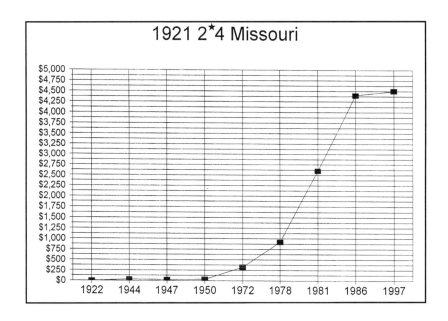

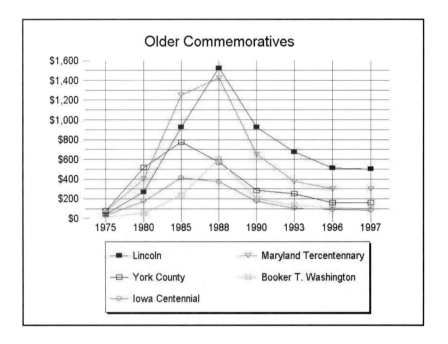

Modern
Commemorative Coins

Let me admit it from the start: I like modern commemorative coins. They are interesting, they are historic, their designs are artistic, most of the events they commemorate are real rather than imagined and—this is heresy—many of them will turn out to be good long-term investments.

My views are unorthodox—at least at this time. Here is a prediction that I'm betting my reputation on: uncirculated modern commemorative coin issues will turn out to be the giant sleeper of contemporary numismatics and will outperform virtually any other investment in your rare coin retirement portfolio, provided that you make your purchases on the secondary market.

An important caveat: please understand my background, how I have made this analysis and where I am coming from. For fifteen years, together with some other hobby leaders, I was a voice in the wilderness arguing strenuously for a return to commemorative coinage, without the abuses that were associated with the former system that the mint managed between 1892 and 1954. I wrote on this topic ceaselessly and extensively and argued that there was a market for modern commemorative coins—provided that the programs were run the correct way.

I was present at the congressional hearing in May, 1981, when U.S. Treasurer Angela M. "Bay" Buchanan reversed a sixty-year policy of Treasury opposition and announced that in 1982, the department would issue a commemorative coin honoring the 250th anniversary of the birth of George Washington.

Since then I have attended and testified at many congressional hearings on various species of commemorative coin legislation that were pending. The latest was in July, 1995, and was designed as a general oversight hearing on modern commemorative coins, but resulted in the subsequent enactment of a pet project, for which I have carried a torch for many years: circulating commemorative coins.

Circulating commemorative coins do not belong in your rare coin retirement portfolio (proofs are another story, however). You may want to collect them, but investing in them for the long term should not be your goal. But the interest that these new coins will generate has a great deal to do with why I believe contemporary commemorative coinage has a place in your rare coin retirement.

The statistics are interesting and they show that over $1.5 billion in modern commemorative coin sales have taken place from 1982 through 1996, with many more programs waiting in the wings. The statistics also show that almost without exception, uncirculated coin issues are not preferred by the buyers, who purchase proofs nearly four times more often than the uncirculated version of the coin.

This is right out of the starting block, of course, and means that when collectors make a purchase by mail from the United States Mint, they overwhelmingly buy the proof coin rather than the uncirculated model. There are certainly lots of reasons for this, one of which is that the proof coins are actually more attractive. Their mirror-like surface reflects the beauty of the design, the double-striking that is part of the proof process brings the design to a crystal-clear finish that is more visually appealing.

But coins for your rare coin retirement need to offer something more: investment potential, which is derived based on mintage. The fewer coins there are, the greater the possibility of an increase in value. Of course, if the mintage of proof and uncirculated are nearly the same the proof will almost always outperform the uncirculated because the proofs remain more desirable. However, if there is a wide disparity of mintage, the collector many times will go for the lower-minted uncirculated coin and ignore the proof. There is evidence of this: consider the example of the Barber half dollars from 1892 to 1915. The truly uncirculated coins substantially outperform the proof specimens, even though the proof specimens have a very low mintage.

From looking at contemporary commemorative coinage, it is clear that the uncirculated items that always have low mintages, and the proofs higher mintages. The marketplace has not yet caught up with the fact that the uncirculated coins are the really scarce ones because in some cases the mintages figures are not well established or easily obtainable. The *1998 Guidebook of United States Coins,* published in July, 1997, lists complete mintages only for those coins produced through 1994. The lists for 1995 and 1996 (and, of course, 1997) are incomplete, or not included at all.

Below is a table of commemorative half dollars, dollars, $5 gold pieces and $10 gold pieces produced over the last fifteen years. It has the date, mint mark, denomination, a general description, total mintage, proof mintage, uncirculated mintage and the percentage allocated of each. It's a fair bet that from this chart you will be able to divine some genuine rarities that belong in your rare coin retirement plan.

Coin	Total Mintage	Proof	% Proof	Uncirculated	% Uncirculated	Authorized in millions	% Authorized
1982 Washington 50¢	7,104,502	4,894,044	68.89%	2,210,458	31.11%	10.000	71.05%
1986 Statue of Liberty 50¢	8,853,635	6,925,627	88.18%	928,008	11.83%	10.000	78.54%
1989 Congressional Bicentennial 50¢	897,401	762,198	84.93%	135,203	15.07%	4.000	22.44%
1991 Mt. Rushmore 50¢	926,011	753,257	81.34%	172,754	18.66%	2.500	37.04%
1992 Columbus 50¢	525,973	390,255	74.20%	135,718	25.80%	6.000	8.77%
1992 Olympic 50¢	678,484	517,318	76.25%	161,166	23.75%	6.000	11.31%
1993 Madison 50¢	779,661	586,315	75.20%	193,346	24.80%	1.000	77.97%
1994 World Cup 50¢	777,515	609.172	78.35%	168,343	21.65%	5.000	15.55%

Coin	Total Mintage	Proof	% Proof	Uncirculated	% Uncirculated	Authorized in millions	% Authorized
1994 WW II 50¢	512,759	313,801	61.20%	198,958	38.80%	2.000	25.64%
1995 Civil War 50¢	434,789	322,245	74.12%	112,544	25.88%	2.000	21.74%
1995 Olympic 50¢ Basketball	336,484	165.545	49.20%	170,939	50.80%	2.000	16.82%
1995 Olympic 50¢ Baseball	278,379	114,297	41.06%	164,082	58.94%	2.000	13.92%
1996 Olympic 50¢ Swimming	183,036	135,780	74.18%	47,256	25.82%	2.000	9.15%
1996 Olympic 50¢ Soccer	137,339	88,233	64.24%	49,106	35.76%	2.000	6.87%
1983 Olympic $1	2,219,596	1,577,025	71.05%	642,571	28.95%	50.000	4.44%
1984 Olympic $1	2,252,514	1,801,210	79.96%		20.04%	50.000	4.51%
1986 Statue of Liberty $1	7,138,273	6,414,638	89.86%	723,635	10.14%	10.000	71.38%
1987 Constitution $1	3,198,745	2,747,116	85.88%	451,629	14.12%	10.000	31.99%
1988 Olympic $1	1,550,734	1,359,366	87.66%	191,368	12.34%	10.000	15.51%
1989 Congress $1	931,650	767,897	82.42%	17.58%	3.000	31.06%	
1990 Eisenhower $1	1,386,130	1,144,461	82.57%	241,669	17.43%	4.000	34.65%
1991 Korea $1	831,537	618,488	74.38%	213,049	25.62%	1.000	83.15%
1991 Mt. Rushmore $1	871,558	738,419	84.72%	133,139	15.28%	2.500	34.86%
1991 USO $1	446,233	321,275	72.00%	124,958	28.00%	1.000	44.62%
1992 Columbus $1	492,252	385,290	78.27%	106,962	21.73%	4.000	12.31%
1992 Olympic $1	688,842	503,239	73.06%	185,603	26.94%	4.000	17.22%
1992 White House $1	498,753	375,154	75.22%	123,599	24.78%	0.500	99.75%
1993 Madison $1	632,384	534,001	84.44%	98,383	15.56%	0.900	70.26%
1994 Jefferson	599,818	332,891	55.50%	266,927	44.50%	0.600	99.97%
1994 World Cup $1	658,676	576,978	87.60%	81,698	12.40%	5.000	13.17%
1994 World War II $1	417,130	322,422	77.30%	94,708	22.70%	1.000	41.71%
1994 POW $1	274,890	220,100	80.07%	54,790	19.93%	0.500	54.98%
1994 Vietnam $1	283,579	226,262	79.79%	57,317	20.21%	0.500	56.72%
1994 Women in Military	266,255	213,201	80.07%	53,054	19.93%	0.500	53.25%
1994 Capitol Bicentennial $1	341,619	279416	81.79%	68,352	20.01%	0.500	68.32%
1995 Civil War Battle $1	374,393	324,339	86.63%	50,054	15.43%	1.000	37.44%
1995 Olympic $1-Blind Runner	166,059	137,610	82.87%	28,449	20.67%	0.750	22.14%

Coin	Total Mintage	Proof	% Proof	Uncirculated	% Uncirculated	Authorized in millions	% Authorized
1995 Olympic $1 Gymnast	213,084	171,048	80.27%	42,036	24.58%	0.750	28.41%
1995 Olympic $1 Track	153,706	129,492	84.25%	24,214	18.70%	0.750	20.49%
1995 Olympic $1 Cycling	135,325	115,297	85.20%	20,028	17.37%	0.750	18.04%
1995 Special Olympic	445,019	355,847	79.96%	89,172	25.06%	0.800	55.63%
1996 Olympic $1 Tennis	101,282	85,875	84.79%	15,407	17.94%	0.350	28.94%
1996 Olympic $1 Rowing	125,156	109,292	87.32%	15,864	14.52%	0.500	25.03%
1996 Olympic $1 High Jump	140,596	124,513	88.56%	16,083	12.92%	0.500	28.12%
1996 Olympic $1 Wheelchair Athlete	85,286	71,152	83.43%	14,134	19.86%	0.350	24.37%
1996 Community Service	122,520	99,400	81.13%	23,120	23.26%	0.800	15.32%
1996 Smithsonian $1	157,209	126,616	80.54%	30,593	24.16%	0.800	19.65%
1986 Statue of Liberty $5	499,261	404,013	80.92%	95,248	19.08%	0.500	99.85%
1987 Constitution $5	865,884	651,659	75.26%	214,225	24.74%	1.000	86.59%
1988 Olympic $5	344,378	281,465	81.73%	62,913	18.27%	1.000	34.44%

1988 Olympic Commemorative Dollar

Coin	Total Mintage	Proof	% Proof	Uncirculated	% Uncirculated	Authorized in millions	% Authorized
1989 Congress $5	211,589	164,690	77.83%	46,899	22.17%	1.000	21.16%
1991 Mt. Rushmore $5	143,950	111,991	77.80%	31,959	22.20%	0.500	28.79%
1991 Columbus $5	104,065	79,734	76.62%	24,331	23.38%	0.500	20.81%
1992 Olympic $5	104,214	76,499	73.41%	27,715	26.59%	0.500	20.84%
1993 Madison $5	101,928	78,654	77.17%	23,274	22.83%	0.300	33.98%
1994 World Cup $5	112,066	89,619	79.97%	22,447	20.03%	5.000	2.24%
1994 WW II $5	90.434	66,837	73.91%	23,597	26.09%	0.300	30.14%
1995 Civil War Battle $5	59,203	47,698	80.57%	11,505	19.43%	0.300	19.73%
1995 Olympic $5 Torch runner	69,625	55,034	79.04%	14,591	20.96%	0.175	39.79%
1995 Olympic $5 Stadium	53,108	42,588	80.19%	10,520	19.81%	0.175	30.35%
1996 Olympic $5 Cauldron	47,926	38,940	81.25%	8,896	18.75%	0.150	31.95%
1996 Olympic $5 Flag Bearer	45,569	35,760	78.47%	9,809	21.53%	0.100	45.57%
1996 Smithsonian $5	30,788	21,840	0.00%	8,948	29.06%	0.800	3.85%
1996 FDR	38,500	27,000		11,500			
1984 $10 Olympic Gold	573,364	497,478	86.76%	75,886		1.000	57.34%

Modern American commemorative coin issues have come of age. By the end of this 1997, there will be more than seventy half dollars, silver dollars, $5, and $10 gold pieces to collect by design, and even more coins if dates and mintmarks are added. Since 1982, when the modern era of U.S. commemoratives began, more than 53 million coins have been struck by the U.S. Mints at Philadelphia, Denver, San Francisco and West Point—compared to 17.6 million commemoratives struck at these mints during the golden commemorative era, 1892-1954. (Of those, after official meltings, fewer than 9.5 million pieces survive amongst all 144 silver issues.)

New issue commemorative coins began in 1981 (with the first issue taking place the following year), when Congress passed

1982 George Washington Commemorative

the first legislation in a generation to have a non-circulating legal tender commemorative coin.

The 250th anniversary of George Washington's birth in 1982 was the theme for that year, and the surprising reversal by the Treasury Department at hearings called to consider the program led the way to a whole series of new issues.

Contemporary issues produced since then cover a bevy of themes. Among them: Capitol Botanical Gardens, Capitol Bicentennial, Civil War battlefields, Columbus quincentennial, community service, congressional bicentennial, Constitution bicentennial, Eisenhower centennial, Franklin D. Roosevelt memorial, Jackie Robinson breaking of color barrier, James Madison-Bicentennial of the Constitution. Others include the Korean War thirty-eighth anniversary, Mount Rushmore fiftieth anniversary,

Olympic Games (1984, 1988, 1992, 1996), Prisoners of War, Revolutionary War Patriots, Smithsonian Sesquicentennial, Special Olympics, Statue of Liberty centennial, Thomas Jefferson 250th anniversary, United Services Organization, Vietnam Veterans, Washington bicentennial, White House bicentennial, women in the military, World Cup soccer, and World War II golden anniversary. Some of the issues are contrived, others extraordinarily appropriate from a historic sense. Each, however, is fully legal tender, and much as some of the earlier commemoratives were mocked when issued, they are widely collected today.

Still, what's surprising is that contemporary collectors haven't studied the minting records closely. If they had, they'd be surprised to find out that some of the modern commemorative coin issues are more scarce than the pieces coming out of the golden age of two generations ago. For the most part, these are uncirculated issues rather than proof. On average, nearly 75 percent of all coins in any given design and series will be proofs, because that's what collectors seem to go after. But the remaining 25 percent actually make for scarce coins that, several years hence, could really become unavailable—and hence are likely to rise in price.

Take the 1996 Olympic swimming coin in uncirculated; just 47,256 coins are reported as being sold. The soccer coin mintage is similarly low at 49,106. The Civil War battlefields gold commemorative of 1995 (uncirculated mintage just 11,505) is low

Examples of some modern commemorative coins

1995 Botanic Garden Commemorative

by any standard. A ready contrast: another example is the 1984-P gold eagle $10 gold piece from the Olympic Games in Los Angeles. Mintage as a proof is only 33,309 pieces (the 1984-D proof is 34,553, also not a bad thought). Take the World Cup soccer commemorative coins—something that millions failed to do that year, despite the optimistic authorization by Congress of some 5 million silver dollars. A total of just 81,698 World Cup silver dollars were struck in 1994. Looking at older commemorative half dollars, the 1926 Oregon trail from 1926 has about 83,000 mintage after melts, or the 1925 California has a mintage of 86,000 pieces left. Then look at the 1994 Prisoner of War commemorative of which only 54,790 are uncirculated specimens. The mintage is around the same as the 1936 Cleveland half (after meltings) or the 1936 Rhode Island—either of which are coins that any collector would like to have.

Prices on the modern commemoratives are good too. Almost as soon as the issue is off-sale from the U.S. Mint, the price drops to reflect the fact that there is no longer a surcharge. (That didn't apply of course to sell outs like the White House commemorative). The result is that today, they are a bargain.

Recent advertisements in *COINage* magazine confirm that contemporary commemorative coins remain a great collecting pattern from the secondary market. For example, New World Rarities of Bohemia, New York, has the World War II half dollar and dollar for sale at $28.50 (uncirculated) and $34.50 (proof). The original issue price was $37 in uncirculated, $41 in proof. Only 94,000 uncirculated silver dollars were manufactured.

Robert Berger Rare Coins, Nesconset, New York, offers the Statue of Liberty $5 gold piece, uncirculated or proof, at $115. The original issue cost was $160 in uncirculated, $170 as a proof specimen. Berger also offers the 1991 USO commemorative in either state at $16.50; the original cost was $23 in uncirculated, $28 as a proof. Mintage was just 124,000 in uncirculated, with a respectable but low mintage 321,000 for proofs.

There are certainly ample reasons to buy from the mint in their direct offerings. That is also the way that the 1997 matte proof Jefferson nickel was available at a bargain price. (The secondary market is trading them at $300 or thereabouts.)

But among the coins themselves, the future seems bright for the earlier issues. The themes are nice, the workmanship sharp, the mintages low, and the upside considerable.

Because nearly all are produced in proof and uncirculated (the early commemoratives for the most part were not produced as proofs), there are well over 125 different modern commemorative coins produced in a very short period of time. There was a problem absorbing the forty-eight different old-style commemoratives at the time of issue because there were too many coins. The same is true now.

Modern commemorative coinage has all of the key char-

acteristics for future growth and thus, it is a very promising investment candidate for your rare coin retirement portfolio. Obviously,
this is not true of every coin. The uncirculated coins, tend to be
better investments than the proof specimens.

Here are some of the coins I believe will prove to be profitable investments.

- White House silver dollar. Only 500,000 were authorized, and most were sold as proof. It celebrates the
bicentennial of the White House, and there is already a good secondary market for this particular
coin. The overall series consists of a single coin, and
even for those not seeking a complete set of contemporary commemorative coins, this is likely to be
one that is included. It celebrates a historic anniversary, is totally American in its theme and its value already surpassed its surcharge of $10.

- [1993–1994] Thomas Jefferson silver dollar. This
marks the 250th anniversary of Jefferson's birth in
1993, though Congress did not approve it until 1994
(albeit with a 1993 date). The uncirculated version
has a mintage of just 266,927, has also sold out a
600,000 total mintage of all coins and seems to have
the "legs" for a major program. Given the good
theme, low mintage and desirability for completion
of even partial collections, this coin has great potential for growth.

- Dwight D. Eisenhower dollar commemorative uncirculated. This 1990 commemorative with conjugate
portraits of Eisenhower as a citizen, and Eisenhower
as a soldier, is the first of modern commemoratives
to honor the centennial of the birth of an American
president. There will eventually be other coins in the
series, making them collectible as well. In the mean-
while, contemporary commemoratives honoring de-

ceased presidents are an attractive set to collect, and this is a good component. In uncirculated, the mintage is just 241,669 of a total of 1,386,130 of pieces struck (17.43 percent of the overall mintage). This coin has good possibilities to help fund your rare coin retirement.

- USO Commemorative silver dollar (1991). The coin commemorating the golden anniversary of the United States Organization, which has taken care of the needs of America's service men and women for two generations, lacks an attractive or unusual design, but its relatively low mintage in uncirculated gives it a greater desirability for your rare coin portfolio. The total mintage was 446,233, and the uncirculated mintage was just 124,958 or 28 percent of the total. It is starting to seem a little contrived, but at least its a fiftieth anniversary. The real rationale for this coin is fund-raising, and in the secondary market this coin is available at a deep discount off the original price of $28. None of that suggests that it won't be a valuable coin in the future.

- Korean War silver dollar. Issued on the thirty-eighth anniversary of the end of the Korean War in 1991, the focus of this coin was the building of the national war memorial. Pundits have suggested that the thirtieth anniversary and the thirty-eighth parallel (separating North and South Korea) make this into some kind of a mystical coin, but the coin's existence is owed to the need for funds by yet another worthwhile charitable organization. The coin is not an artistic success, and the soldiers look artificial. Artificiality aside, the relatively low mintage in uncirculated of 213,049 will reward those willing to use this coin to help plan their rare coin retirement.

- 1996 Wheelchair Athletes silver dollar. This Olympic issue with just 14,143 pieces in uncirculated (85,286 total mintage) has all the clear earmarks of a winner. What other silver dollar has a mintage of only 14,134 in uncirculated condition?

- Civil War Battlefield $5 commemorative. Just 11,505 of these pieces were produced in uncirculated and 59,203 in total. Originally sold at $220 in proof and $200 in uncirculated, prices range from $130 to $140, just outside the range for planning your rare coin retirement. The coin has a good theme, has a low mintage and it looks like a winner.

There are a number of other coins that you might also want to consider for your rare coin retirement, but it is going to take some ingenuity to find them. A safe and profitable approach to collecting contemporary commemorative coins is to consider any mintage that is below 100,000. This makes sense for a lot of rea-

1996 Smithsonian Institute Commemorative

1994 Prisoner of War Commemorative

sons, not the least of which is that below that level, there is a good chance that the demand will exceed the supply. There are, of course, no guarantees but if you look at Peace dollars, the lowest mintage is 361,000 for the 1928 period. Among Morgan silver dollars, the 1893-S at 100,000 is a very scarce coin with values into the tens of thousands of dollars in better grade. (No Morgan silver dollar except for the 1895, with a mintage of 12,880 is available; those pieces that are known are the 1880 proof). In fact, you'd have to go back more than 125 years to the Liberty seated dollars in the 1870's, near the end of the series, before you get such low mintages, and even there, there is awfully good value for the money.

Here is a list of twenty-four modern commemorative coins with mintages of under 100,000 pieces; most of the $1 coins are available well within our budget and the $5 gold coins are available in the $130 to $150 range. An important caveat: during the summer of 1997, buyers may have discovered the great prices in these low-mintage coins, because the advertising of these coins has almost entirely dried up. With some effort, however, they are available in the secondary market.

1996 Community Service	23,120
1933 Madison $5	23,274
1994 WWII $5	23,597
1995 Olympic $1 Track	24,214
1992 Columbus $5	24,331
1992 Olympic $5	27,715
1995 Olympic $1 Blind Runner	28,449
1996 Smithsonian $1	30,593
1991 Mt. Rushmore $5	31,959
1995 Olympic $1 Gymnast	42,036
1989 Congress $5	46,899
1996 Olympics 50¢ Swimming	47,256
1996 Olympic 50¢ Soccer	49,106
1995 Civil War Battle $1	50,054
1994 Women in Military	53,054
1994 POW $1	54,790
1994 Vietnam $1	57,317
1988 Olympic $5	62,913
1994 Capitol Bicentennial $1	68,352
1994 World Cup $1	81,698
1995 Special Olympics $1	89,172
1994 World War II $1	94,708
1986 Statue of Liberty $5	95,248
1993 Madison $1	98,383

Among modern commemoratives, the choice is nearly endless, but each uncirculated example that you acquire today can make a nice, and important contribution to your rare coin retirement tomorrow.

Uncirculated Peace Dollars
(MS-65) (1921-1935) ($112) (MS-64)

America's first circulating commemorative coin designed to celebrate peace was issued for circulation from 1921 to 1935. More than 190 million coins, produced at the Philadelphia, Denver and San Francisco Mints, were manufactured before coinage was suspended in the midst of the Great Depression in 1935. (Though not released into circulation, more than 300,000 were also struck at the Denver mint in 1964 on direct orders of President Johnson. Congress later countermanded the order, the coins were melted, and further issuance of silver dollars was banned until 1970.) There are a number of uncirculated Peace dollars that make a perfect addition to your rare coin retirement portfolio; the only real question is whether to go for quality with this historic coin, or for quantity and value.

At the 1920 ANA convention, the official historian of the ANA, Farran Zerbe, presented a paper entitled *Commemorate the Peace with a Coin for Circulation.* ANA then appointed a five-man committee to propose the bill to Congress. One of the members was Congressman William A. Ashbrook of Ohio.

By December, 1920, they met with Representative Albert Vestal, chairman of the House Committee on Coinage, Weights and Measures, and a joint resolution was presented to Congress on May 9, 1921 calling for the design "commemorative of the termination of the war between the Imperial German Government and the people of the United States." (There was some objection raised to the legislative proposal on the House floor, principally because it called for re-issuing the silver dollar, the minting of which had

Peace Dollar (MS-65)
Photo Credit: Numismatic News/Krause Publications

been suspended in 1904; the Treasury secretary later used his statutory authority to cause the Peace Dollar to be issued.)

Anthony de Francisci was the designer; his young wife, Theresa, was the model for the head on the obverse. The eagle reverse depicts a vigilant eagle cautiously eyeing the horizons as a guardian against war, but the motif allegorically suggesting peace, right down to the olive branch in the eagle's talons.

In planning your rare coin retirement, one goal is obtaining the best possible condition of a coin, while another is to maximize upside potential. Any Peace dollar in MS-65 (the date is dealer's choice) fits the bill as suitable for inclusion in your rare coin retirement portfolio. But so do MS-64 Peace dollars. The reason for this is that each has the potential to grow back and move beyond where they were in 1979 and 1980.

There are several reasons for this. First, fewer than 40,000

Peace dollars have been certified by PCGS and NGC as MS-65, compared with 84,000 in MS-63 and 137,000 in MS-64. Second, at today's price average of about $112, this acts as a contrast with 1989 when $710 was a high price for a comparable coin. So the upside is virtually unlimited.

Peace dollars like the Morgan dollars are large size—38.1mm or one and a half inches in diameter—the largest circulating American coin. No doubt another reason why this series has been popular with investors through the years is that its size makes it easier to grade. The attractive design makes for a nice addition to any collection. There are about half a dozen dates in MS-64 or MS-65 that could be placed in your rare coin retirement portfolio. At $112 a coin or thereabouts, each would make a very nice addition with substantial growth potential.

An alternative choice to consider when planning your rare coin retirement can be found using MS-64 Peace dollars, which can be purchased for about $28. In 1989, their price reached about $180 (to reach that level again would mean a gain of 530 percent). There is not much difference between an MS-64 and MS-65, though the upside on the MS-65 is higher and the percent of possible gain is more. So, it becomes a question of whether you go for the higher graded diversification or perhaps pick both for your rare coin retirement portfolio. That choice is yours.

Dates that you are likely able to include within the budget of the rare coin retirement portfolio include: 1923 MS-65 ($130), and the following in (MS-64): 1922-P, $40; 1922-D, $70; 1923, $40; and the following in MS-63: 1926-S, $57; and 1935, $68.

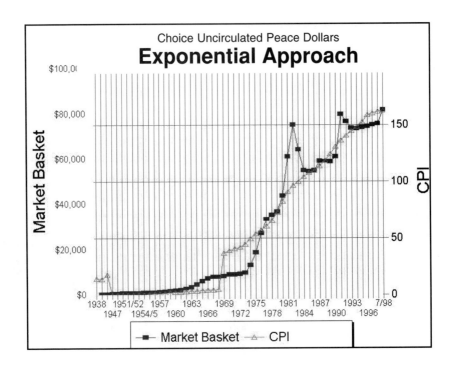

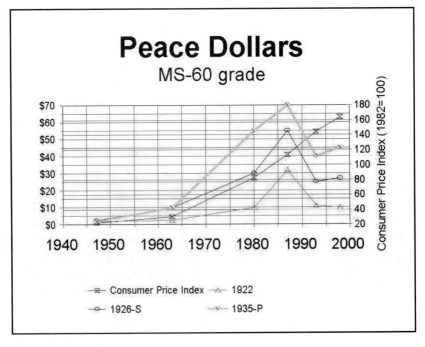

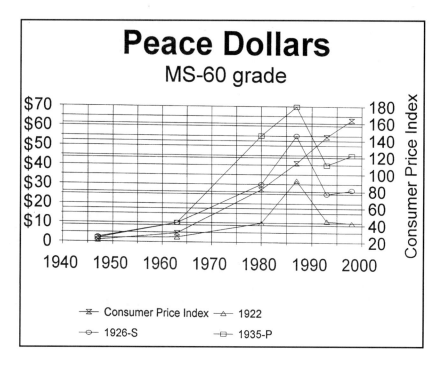

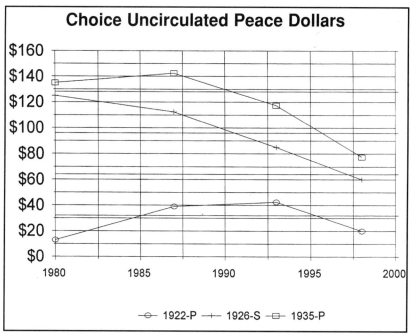

Foreign Gold Coins

Either you want to purchase foreign gold coins for your rare coin retirement, or you don't. It all depends on whether or not you believe in gold as an asset, and think that the price is likely to increase in the future. (Candidly, how could the price of gold get materially lower than it is in 1997?)

There are those who view gold as an expensive asset—something that you cannot easily put into a rare coin retirement plan. They are wrong. The chart that accompanies shows that you could create your own rare coin retirement consisting of 100 gold coins that would cost you $10,000 or less, combined.

If you follow my plan for a rare coin retirement, you'll include a number of gold coins in your portfolio. You have many options, because there are many affordable gold coins that are in the $100 and under price range.

The precise number of gold coins that you do include is up to you. You can take the approach that you want an entirely gold rare coin retirement, or one where you've hedged a little bit and included other coins. It's your choice; it's your retirement.

More than fifty countries are represented on this very incomplete chart of items that you may want to consider for your rare coin retirement. There are over 100 coins listed, nearly all of which cost less than $100; prices that are quoted in the chart are from actual advertisements offering world gold coins for sale from the pages of the monthly newspaper *World Coin News,* the weekly periodical *Numismatic News,* and its competitor, *Coin World.*

Nations from A to Z have all produced low-denomination, low-mintage, highly collectable gold coins that can fit the budget of every collector. Some are available for under $99, many more for less than $150, and hundreds for less than $175 each. (The lowest priced coin on the chart is from Iran, a 1/2 Toman in circulated (very fine) condition, at $39.)

As a precious metal that is virtually indestructible, it has been a storehouse of value from ancient times to the present. For more than 500 years, it has been the coin of choice—which every country of economic significance coined, and until about seventy years ago, circulated widely. In recent times, gold has once again achieved a preeminent coinage role, though not for circulating monies. Instead, it is the metal of choice for commemorative issues because it gives prestige, value, stability, and mystique to modern commemorative coinage sets.

When I started collecting coins some thirty years ago, government regulation was actually quite minimal. Private gold ownership was prohibited in bullion form, and most rare gold coins of foreign origin were prohibited if made in modern times—initially defined by the regulators as meaning post-1933 issues.

The primary regulators were in the Office of Domestic Gold and Silver Operations (ODGSO), located deep within the bowels of the Treasury Department. The ODGSO was first headed by Dr. Leland Howard, and later by Thomas W. Wolfe, who I interviewed for the first time in 1968, long before Americans regained the right to own gold. (At the time, a free-market for gold had just been established abroad that was not tied to the single price of $35 an ounce, that had existed since 1934's evaluation of the dollar).

Within the span of just a couple of years, Congress smashed the regulation that enumerated the gold coins that could and could not be imported into the United States. The regulations never made much sense anyway and seemed arbitrary by the most objective of standards.

According to the regulation, each item included on the list of coins permitted to be imported was required to be both "rare and unusual." Rarity, at least in modern times, is frequently predicated on mintage and condition, yet, while the Treasury Department declared that a 1958 gold sovereign (mintage 8.7 million pieces) was eligible for admission under ODGSO guidelines, a 1962 sovereign (mintage 3 million pieces) was not eligible. "Old Doc Howard wouldn't tell anybody what the standards were," Harvey G. Stack of Stack's related to me recently. He apparently simply revelled in the power of being able to grant, or deny the right of a collector or dealer to import one gold coin or another.

Stack belives the reason the rules were revised and changed after several years of battling was that the Treasury based its determination not on mintage or condition, but on the valuation listed in the Friedberg *Gold Coins of the World* catalogue. If the item was more than 125 percent of its gold value, it was deemed "rare," even if it sold for a lot more. If the *Standard Catalogue* (which identified by type, not date) did not show it, the coin was deemed inadmissible.

The Office of Domestic Gold and Silver Operations passed into history with the legalization of private gold ownership, but the regulation of gold has certainly continued: even the very type of gold produced by the U.S. Mint has been extensively regulated by Congress.

Back in 1978, when private gold ownership was still relatively new, a proposal was made to create what ultimately resulted in the American Arts gold medallion pieces. Some saw the possibility that these medallions could be pseudo-coins, while other visionaries such as Grover Criswell, then-president of the American Numismatic Association, argued strenuously before Congress that they could replace the krugerrand, if only they were given a chance.

Treasury Department experts, and one former high Treasury official, Dr. Edward Bernstein, then a private consultant, strongly recommended against placing any of the magic words that are associated with legal tender on the medallions. It was simply deemed potentially too disruptive to the world of finance, which seems ridiculous in 1990, especially given the involvement of virtually every major power in selling, or attempting to sell, gold coinage. But in the heady days of the Carter administration, government regulation and congressional involvement had run amuck.

That the resulting medallions were able to be sold at all is simply a tribute to American ingenuity, since it was apparent that the Treasury Department, and the mint, not only vigorously op-posed their issue, but also did all that was possible afterwards to sabotage their possible success.

The unscrupulous of the Middle East, and elsewhere, were taking a nominal amount of gold (accurate in fineness, and weight), a good set of newly made dies, and manufacturing their own "coins" which were then sold to the gullible. The potential for profit was enormous, both as a percentage and in terms of the dol-lars actually involved. A U.S. $20 gold piece is an example. Each $20 gold coin contained .9675 troy ounces of gold, and when measured at the official rate of $35 an ounce, contained $33.86 worth of gold. By converting the lump of gold into a coin, a coun-terfeiter was able to sell it for at least $48 (a profit of $15 per coin) or more than 45 percent of cost. Not bad work, even if it was ille-gal, especially since it was generally not illegal in most of the countries where this took place.

The Bureau of Customs, and their ubiquitous customs agents, were a line of first defense, and the Office of Domestic Gold and Silver Operations guidelines were meant as much for their assistance as to prohibit collectors from owning rare and un-usual coins. Even today, the customs agents are responsible for en-forcing a number of laws and regulations, and are a real friend to the hobbyist.

Ultimately, it was the Customs Bureau that found violations of the Hobby Protection Act and prevented the importation and in-troduction into interstate commerce of unauthorized reproductions of numismatic items that did not bear the word "copy" on them.

Even as gold has reached historic, contemporary lows, the metal still remains (in historical context and perspective) a rela-tively good value. Put differently, it may not have been a good in-vestment between 1980 and 1992, but when the prices are viewed over the last fifty or sixty years, you can see that gold has had an astonishing return.

The price of gold, in 1837, was $20.67 an ounce. At that level, a $10 gold piece had $9.99 worth of gold in it. Later, a $20 gold piece became the cornerstone to the system, weighing in

Queen Elizabeth's portrait has been changed four times during her reign, which began in 1952 after the death of King George VI. The fourth change became effective beginning in 1998.

with nearly an ounce of gold (actually .9675 troy ounces) worth its nominal value.

Some ninety-six years after the Coinage Act of January 18, 1837, was passed, the nation was mired in depression, and on the verge of financial calamity. Gold ownership was banned in an attempt to alleviate the depression. The plan failed, but monetary policy regulation remained in the United States for the next half century.

It took forty-one years before the right to own gold coins was restored; in the interim, rare and unusual gold coins were per-

mitted to be acquired by collectors. This included not only domestic coins, but those minted abroad.

There was a black market that existed for post-1960 coins
but the problem was never massive because the intrinsic value of
gold made it difficult to collect coins in quantity. But collecting by
type was and is popular—whether it is by portrait of British rulers,
by first year of issue, last year of issue, or geographically.

British rulers on sovereigns or half sovereigns in the twentieth century include Elizabeth II, George VI, Edward VII, and Vic-
toria. These coins can be purchased for between $70 and $150,
depending on condition. Even a 1/3 Guinea of King George III, the
German speaking monarch who lost the colonies, can be had in
XF for a mere $150.

Suppose you wanted a collection of single gold coins, from
various countries in Europe. A 10 pesetos with the portrait of Al-
fonso XII is widely available in uncirculated for less than $100. A
5 franc of Napoleon III can be obtained in VF/VI for as little as
$50. Germany's Kaiser Wilhelm II on a 20 mark coin (.1867 troy
ounces of gold) is available in uncirculated in the $150 range, as
is a one year type from Greece, the 1884-A 20 Drachmai of King
George I. A 20 Lire of Italy's King Umberto I from 1882 sells for
barely more than its weight in gold in uncirculated at about $95,
while a Swedish 10 kronor 1883 in BU costs about $135. A more
modern, and less expensive coin, is a Polish 10 zlotych in AU at
about $90 while a Serbian 10 dinara of 1882 in VF is in the $110
range. Denmark's 20 kroner of 1917 in BU is a $110 item, while
a 1970 Albanian 50 leke costs about $125 in proof, even though
a mere 500 pieces were minted. A coin such as the Netherlands 1
ducat of 1928 in BU costs about $65 while another one year type
of the Russian 7 1/2 ruble of Nicholas II (1897) is a $110 item in
VF condition. Many of these coins come from an era when gold
was king of international monetary finance, and a linchpin in the
monetary systems of nations throughout the world.

Gold became, at least in the United States, a dominant political issue; some say that the valuation of gold, and the free
coinage of silver was the major campaign issue in every presiden-

tial election during the last quarter of the nineteenth century. It was in this debate that William Jennings Bryan cried that mankind should not be "crucified upon a cross of gold."

By 1900, the Gold Standard was, in fact, proclaimed by the United States, and honored by nations the world over. A review of the Annual Report of the Director of the Mint for the various fiscal years shows a steady shipment and receipt of gold coins from all over the world by the United States. Many of these coins stayed in commerce, to be acquired by collectors. Others were swept up in the gold recall of 1933, though many were saved as collectibles.

Once the Great Depression began, world governments began to limit the rights of their citizens to own gold because it permitted the holder more of a voice in their economic destiny. The American prohibition was more absolute than many, but there were severe restrictions imposed on ownership, transfer, import, and export of gold in many countries.

Americans were still able to own gold if they were coin collectors. That was the loophole written into the regulations. It was intentional, for the law was not meant to be a measure aimed at the nation's coin collectors, it was meant for the hoarders or speculators.

Modern anomalies aside, gold's 200-year history shows a strong stability. In January, 1837, the United States Congress passed, and President Andrew Jackson signed into law, legislation that effectively put the nation on a gold standard. Priced at $20.67 an ounce, gold stayed at that level, except for very occasional blips, for almost a century. In 1933, with the nation in the depths of depression, President Franklin D. Roosevelt devalued the dollar by executive order, increasing the price of gold by nearly 60 percent to $35 an ounce. There the price stayed until March, 1968, even against runs on the dollar, during which the United States pledged to redeem every dollar presented by a foreign government for gold at the $35 per troy ounce rate.

President Johnson ended the gold standard in 1968, and it floated up and down, actually declining on January 16, 1970 to

$34.95 an ounce. But it then began the inevitable march upward, and by March 15, 1971, President Nixon devalued the dollar again, allowing it to rise to $38 an ounce. By 1972, the price was devalued yet again to $42.22 an ounce, which is still the official price of gold.

The bulk of gold in the world is held by nation's central banks. According to the World Gold Council statistics, more than 900 million troy ounces are held by governments, and of that about 85 percent is held by industrialized countries.

The Statistical Abstract of the United States, a government publication, quoting the Board of Governors of the Federal Reserve System, states that since 1983, the United States has had about $11.1 billion worth of gold valued at $42.22 an ounce. That translates to about 262 million troy ounces, or about a third of the gold in the industrialized world.

Gold's price is more than mere speculation; there is a genuine industrial demand, a requirement for jewelry, and increasingly, for coinage. The world's largest market for gold is, surprisingly, India, which used 415 tons in 1994; the U.S. was second with a demand for 312 tons. Each ton contains 2,000 pounds, and each pound contains 12 troy ounces, so U.S. usage amounts to about 7.4 million troy ounces.

Other key countries that utilize gold are Japan (229 tons), the People's Republic of China (224 tons), South Arabia (162 tons), Taiwan (162 tons), Italy (109 tons), South Korea (106 tons), Indonesia (97 tons), Turkey and Germany (81 tons each), and then a hodge podge of other lesser weights for other nations. Europe overall uses slightly more gold than the United States does—339 tons to 306 in 1993, 336 tons to 311 in 1994.

All this adds up to significant demand for the metal, which is now driving the price. Mines that produce gold have been shutting down because of high operating costs, and that, too, tends to start to constrict supply.

American collectors and investors have become fascinated with gold, perhaps because of the long period during which it was forbidden fruit. Once gold ownership was again legal, Congress initially resisted issuing coinage. Gold medallions were used instead, because the Federal Reserve and experts predicted that gold coinage would disrupt the domestic and international monetary system. It never happened.

By 1985, the American eagle gold coin had been introduced, and it proved wildly successful: more than 5 million one ounce coins, 1.1 million half ounce coins, and a total of more than 10.8 million pieces (plus 2.4 million proof pieces) were minted in the course of the first ten years of the Eagle program.

Significantly, the popularity of these coins surged, and the Eagles displaced the krugerrand, and later the Canadian Maple Leaf as the American bullion coin of choice.

What is astonishing—and shows America's interest in gold—is that the five million one ounce coins were essentially sold into a down market. More were sold in 1995. (Ironically, 1994 one ounce pieces with a mintage of 200,000 are at a record low and could actually constitute a collectible rarity on their own.)

The accompanying chart shows gold coins from more than fifty countries at moderate prices available. The prices are so low that there is literally almost no downside risk—unless the price of gold totally collapses. (Then you are forced to rely on the face value of the coin.)

There are many others that are not on this list that are also available, which if added to your portfolio, could well help you plan your rare coin retirement.

Contemporary foreign gold and platinum issues have profit potential

An Important Guide for World Gold Coin Buffs

Essential to any world gold coin buff is Friedberg's *Gold Coins of the World*, sixth edition, published at $55 by the Coin & Currency Institute, Clifton, New Jersey, Containing 723 pages it lists coinage by country and type, each of which is assigned a numismatic number.

By looking at a catalog number for any gold coin in an advertisement, an article or on a dealer's flip, a collector instantly knows a great deal about a coin. For example, a Bulgaria FR-3 means that the coin is 20 leva denomination; a one year type issued only in 1894. A separate table gives the weight and fineness of thousands of gold coin issues.

The book is in many libraries, including that of the American Numismatic Association, and is widely available from dealers who stock numismatic supplies.

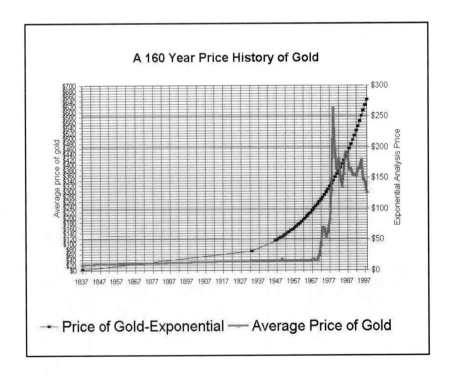

A 160 Year Price History of Gold

Price of Gold-Exponential — Average Price of Gold

World Gold Coin Portfolio with Selected Platinum Issues

Country	Coin		Condition	Price
Australia	1896	Sovereign	Unc.	$110.00
Austria	1881A	8 Florin/20 Franc	XF	$87.00
Austria		1 Ducat	XF-AU	$43.95
Austria	1915	1 Ducat (restrike)	BU	$42.95
Bahamas	1974	$100	Proof	$130.00
Barbados	1975	$100	Proof	$60.00
Belgium		20 Francs	XF-AU	$70.00
Belize	1981	$100 national Independence	Pf	$125.00
Belize	1981	$50	Proof	$40.00
Belize	1985	$100	Proof	$45.00
Bermuda	1975	$100	Proof	$105.00
Bermuda	1977	$50	Proof	$75.00
Bolivia	1952	7 gRAMOS	BU	$95.00
Brit. Virgin Islands	1981	$50	Proof	$55.00
Brit. Virgin Islands	1975	$100	Proof	$100.00
Bulgaria	1894	10 Leva	VF	$100.00
Canada		1/14 oz. Maple Leaf	BU or Pf	$57.50
Canada		1/10 oz Platinum Maple Leaf	BU	$52.65
Canada	1987	Olympic	$100 proof	$99.00
Canada		1/10 oz Platinum Lynx	$30 proof	$109.95
Canada	1989	Indian		$102.00
Canada	1976	Olympic	$100 unc	$94.00
Canada	1997	Maple leaf 1/4 oz		$96.50
Cayman Islands		$25	BU	$83.00
Columbia	1913	5 Pesos	AU	$105.00
Comoros	1976	10,000 Francs	Pf	$125.00
Cook Islands	1975	$100	Proof	$130.00
Cook Islands	1988	Bison	Proof	$45.00
Cuba	1916	2 Peso	BU	$119.00
Egypt	1930	100 Piastres	AU	$100.00
El Salvador	1971	50 Colonies	Proof	$100.00
El Salvador	1971	25 Colonies	Proof	$75.00
Equatorial Guinea	1970	250 Pesetas	Proof	$100.00
Finland	1882	100 Maarka	BU	$99.00
France	1801	(AN 12A) 20 Francs	VF	$125.00
France	1815	20 Fr Bordeaux Louis XVIII	VF	$115.00
France	1814	20 Francs	XF	$95.00
France	1886	20 Francs (3d Republic)	AU	$78.00
France		20 Francs	XF-AU	$70.00
France		20 Franc Rooster (1899-1914)	BU	$79.95
France	1856	A 5 Francs	VF	$51.00
Germany		10 Marks	BU	$115.00
Germany		20 Mark	XF/AU	$84.50
Gibralter	1997	Classical heads (set of 4)		$198.00
Great Britain		Sovereign Eliz. II	XF-AU	$84.00
Great Britain		Sovereign Old style	XF-AU	$87.00
Great Britain	1989	Sovereign	Proof	$100.00
Great Britain	1986	1/2 Sovereign	Proof	$61.00

Country	Coin		Condition	Price
Guernsey	1981	£1	Proof	$125.00
Guinea	1970	1000 Francs	Proof	$125.00
Guyana	1976	$100	Proof	$50.00
Haiti	1973	200 Gourdes	Proof	$75.00
Haiti	1973	100 Gourdes	Proof	$60.00
Hungary	1885	20 Fr/8 Florin	XF	$82.00
India	1918	Sovereign	BU	$105.00
Iran	AH1322	5000 Dinars	XF	$75.00
Iran	AH1342	1/2 Toman	VF-XF	$39.00
Iran	1971	500 Rials (Fr 109)	Pf	$125.00
Italy		20 Lire	XF-AU	$68.00
Jamaica	1975	$100	Proof	$100.00
Japan	1835	2 Shu	XF	$52.00
Liberia	1977	$100	Proof	$125.00
Luxembourg	1953	20 Francs (KM #1M)	BU	$100.00
Malaysia	1976	200 Ringgit	Pf	$100.00
Malta	1974	20 Pounds	Proof	$90.00
Malta	1974	10 Pounds	Proof	$60.00
Mexico		2 Pesos	BU	$24.95
Mexico	1906	5 Pesos	Unc.	$55.00
Mexico	1946	2 1/2 Pesos	BU	$42.00
Mexico	1905	10 Pesos	XF-AU	$99.00
Mexico		5 Pesos	BU	$43.00
Mexico		10 Pesos	BU	$82.50
Mexico		2 1/2 Pesos	BU	$32.95
Mexico	1985	250 Pesos	BU	$99.00
Netherlands		10 Guilder	XF-AU	$72.50
Netherlands	1988	2 Ducats	Proof	$120.00
Netherlands	1975	1 Ducat	Proof	$60.00
Netherlands Antilles	1979	50 Guilden	BU	$40.00
Panama	1975	100 Balboas	Proof	$90.00
Papua New Guinea	1975	100 Kina	Proof	$110.00
Peru	1965	100 Soles	BU	$65.00
Russia		5 Rubles Nicholas II	XF-AU	$47.95
South Africa	1964	Proof Set	Proof	$135.00
South Africa		2 Rands (1962-83) 1/4 oz	BU	$88.00
South Africa	1894	1/2 Pond	VF	$75.00
South Africa	1982	Krugerrand 1/10 oz	BU	$42.95
Spain	1878	Alfonso XII (Fr 343R)	BU	$85.00
Sudan	1978	25 Pounds (Fr 4)	Pf	$135.00
Switzerland		20 Francs	XF-AU	$70.00
Switzerland		10 Francs	XF-AU	$100.00
Turkey	1969	50 Kurish	MS64	$75.00
Turks & Caicos	1976	50 Crowns	Proof	$100.00
Turks & Caicos	1981	100 Crowns	Proof	$90.00
Turks & Caicos	1976	25 Crowns	Proof	$75.00
USA	1987	Constitution $5 commemorative	BU or Pf	$99.00
USA	1997	Gold 1/10 oz Eagle	BU	$43.00
USA	1997	Gold 1/4 oz Eagle	BU	$96.00
USA	1988	Olympic $5	BU or Pf	$99.00

Country	Coin		Condition	Price
USA		$1 Type 1 (1849-1854)	VF	$103.00
USA		$1 Type 3 (1856-1889)	VF	$107.00
USA		$2 1/2 Indian (1908-1929)	VF	$119.00
Venezuela	1905	20 Bolivares (Fr 6)	MS-64	$100.00
Venice	1789	Zecchino (Fr. 1445)	VF-XF	$155.00
Yugoslavia	1982	5000 Dinara	Pf	$100.00

Platinum Coins for Your Rare Coin Retirement

Platinum. Its shiny, silvery color has held a fascination all its own for centuries, making for some unusual and rare coins in the process. If gold is the precious metal that grabs the financial press headlines, there's another, even more precious metal that has moved to the forefront in recent years both as an investment vehicle (in the form of one ounce bullion coins and fractionals) and for pure numismatic appeal: platinum.

There's a correlation between coin prices, stock prices, and precious metal prices. And even in the bull stock market of 1997-8, rare coins and platinum bullion coinage are outperforming all expectations for tangible assets.

This performance record can be seen in fractional bullion items (uncirculated platinum pieces such as the 1/2 ounce, 1/4 ounce, 1/10 ounce and 1/20 ounce) produced by a number of countries, as well as in the one ounce bullion pieces, whose future has been secured by United States entry into the platinum coinage field in 1997.

Significantly, fractional proof (collector-only) platinum issues have developed a significant after market, which portends a bright future, and makes them the type of piece that you might want to consider for your rare coin retirement.

Platinum in Historical Perspective

One of the heaviest substances known, about 21 times the weight of water of the same volume, it is easy to shape like gold and silver, does not tarnish, and has been used for coinage for more than two centuries.

Chemically described platinum is the 78th element on the periodic table has a high density of 21.5 grams per cubic centimeter, a melting point of 1,772 degrees centigrade (3,224 degrees Fahrenheit), and is the most valuable impurity of most nickel deposits where with the other platinum medals of ruthenium, palladium, osmium, and iridium it is among the rarest of metals, and scarcest of coins.

Discovered by Italian scientist Julius Scaliger in 1557, large quantities of the metal were not available until about 1750, when the Spaniards found platinum in Peru. They named it platinum from their word "plata," which means silver. Miners frequently refer to it as white gold because it can be found in beds of gold-bearing sand.

Like gold, it can be found in nugget form; in 1843, a twenty-one pound lump was found in Russia, which regularly issued platinum coinage from 1828-1845 in the 3, 6 and 12 ruble denominations. These coins are quite rare today and are avidly sought by collectors.

Just sixty-four years after platinum's major commercial availability began, the United States Mint produced its first pattern coin, a half dollar dated 1814 described by Dr. Judd in his book *United States Pattern, Experimental & Trial Pieces* (Judd #44) as an experimental piece from regular dies.

Only three specimens are known (the coin is Rarity 8); one piece is "defaced with 33 Ps punched in the field on the obverse and the word "Platina" is engraved on the reverse," Judd writes. Earlier, Adams and Woodin's book on patterns (1913) called this coin (AW-29) a unique specimen in the collection of Chicago beer baron Virgil Brand.

There was also one without the punched letters (AW-30) in the Philadelphia Mint collection (now part of the Smithsonian Institution's national coin collection). Interestingly, Adams and Woodin write that, "So far as known, however, there has never been any consideration of the use of the metal for coinage by the United States government."

What was true then changed dramatically in 1997 when Congress enacted legislation that created a platinum bullion coin of high face value, and a proof counterpart that was intended primarily for coin collectors.

Snowden's classic 1859 work, *A Description of Ancient and Modern Coins in the Cabinet of the United States* notes that, "A platina piece struck from the dies for the legal half dollar of that year. It was an experiment, platina being then a new metal . . ."

Although Russia is generally credited with being the first modern coinage of platinum, a search through the archives of *The Numismatist*, the monthly publication of the American Numismatic Association, finds a reference in May, 1917, to a two real pieces of Peru dated 1729, struck on an irregular planchet from platinum metal.

Since then, dozens of other countries the world over have produced coinage in platinum. When the Edwards Medcalf collection was sold by Superior in October, 1987, it was probably the largest single auction of a platinum coinage holding ever acquired. The catalog is an invaluable source to any researcher in the field. "Continuing into the 1950s through the 1970s, he was very active as a buyer. He added more platinum to his already impressive collection," the catalog notes.

Among the Metcalf coins not otherwise generally known as platinum pieces is a 25 dinars of Andorra dated 1960 (type of Krause-Mishler 1), and comparable for 1963, 1964, and 1965. Yet despite the rarity—just two pieces in platinum are known—the prices were very reasonable: from $484 to $577.50.

Other countries' platinum coinage represented included: Bhutan (1966 set, one of seventy-two produced), a Bolivian 8 escudos from 1782 (Potosi mint), a Columbian 8 escudos of 1801, Denmark, France, Germany-Prussia, Britain, Haiti, Hawaii, India, Iran, Isle of Man, Italy, Japan, Lesotho, Liechtenstein, Macao, Madagascar, Mexico, Monaco, Panama, Poland, Russia, Spain (4 and 8 escudos), Switzerland, Tonga, and Venezuela.

There are others that Metcalf missed, including Bhutan

(1979 5 sertums), Portugal, a Dominican Republic 1991 issue celebrating the 50th anniversary of the Columbian voyages, Turks and Caicos commemorative honoring the 25th anniversary of the lunar landing and coin collecting (struck with the ANA).

But, there are now also many other countries that participate in the platinum coinage field. First among them now is the United States. Among the others: Canada, China, Mexico, Australia, Isle of Man, and Russia.

Demand for platinum continues at an all time high. Some 4.5 million ounces were utilized during calendar year 1994, an increase of 11 percent over the previous year. There is considerable industrial use for the metal. Over 5.2 million ounces were utilized in 1997. Of these, an unexpected 105,000 ounces came from the U.S. bullion program (comprising both the uncirculated and proof coin issues).

Jewelry uses for platinum account only for about two million ounces (or about 40 percent of the total demand). Use in automobiles (catalytic converters) accounts for another 1.7 million ounces. Other industries require about 1.5 million ounces of platinum annually. High technology and environmental applications accounted for almost 800,000 ounces last year.

Coin investment products in bullion coins remain a relatively modest 155,000 ounces (outside the new U.S. coinage), principally coming from Canadian Maple Leaf and Australian Koala platinum issues in the United States. The U.S. program nearly doubles that amount.

Sources for platinum and its ancillary product, palladium, are limited; only a handful of countries mine and produce it. The world's largest platinum producer is South Africa, which sold about 3.16 million ounces last year. Russia sold about 1.01 million ounces in 1994.

Platinum is mined principally as an off product of other metal acquisition; a significant amount comes from nickel. Canadian ore principally comes from International Nickel Company (Inco), which last year pulled 2,650 tons a day from the mine to yield 200,000 ounces of platinum and 410,000 ounces of palladium.

The mathematics of this are mind-boggling. This means that 967,250 tons (1.9 billion pounds) of ore (rock and metal) had to be moved in order to recover 16,666 pounds of platinum and about double that amount of palladium.

U.S. production of platinum and palladium is presently limited to a single facility, the Stillwater mine at Nye in the Beartooth mountains of Montana. Recently, a total of 373,000 tons of ore were mined, yielding 63,000 ounces of platinum and 207,000 ounces of palladium.

Bringing the metal to the surface is difficult; the metal is hardly alluvial. At Stillwater, a current plan is to sink a new shaft a third of a mile into the earth, aimed at doubling current production.

As scarce a metal as platinum is, it remains a metal that has been involved in contemporary coinage both for commemorative purposes, and also as an investment vehicle, principally in one ounce and half and quarter ounce increments. Tenth and twentieth of an ounce coins are generally intended for jewelry, though proof versions have become a profitable numismatic venture for collectors.

Besides the major pieces in the Edwards Metcalf collection, here's a handy chart of current platinum coinage that is generally available at only a modest premium over the price of its bullion content. These coins are easily collectible, and relatively speaking, have modest mintages. They afford a bright future for any collector:

Non Circulating Legal Tender Platinum and Palladium Coins
Platinum Coins
Investor Coins—Low Premium Bullion Coins

Country	Name of Coin	Sizes	Issue Date(s)	Comments
Australia	Koala	1, .5, .25, .1 oz.	1988 - Present	Yearly design changes
Australia	Koala	1 Kilo, 10 oz., 2 oz.	1993 - Present	Large Bullion Coins
Canada	Maple Leaf	1, .5, .25, .1 oz.	1988 - Present	Collector
Isle of Man	Noble	1, .5, .25, .1 oz.	1983 - Present	Coins -
Isle of Man	Cat	1, .5, .2, .1, .04 oz.	1989 - Present	Selected
United States	Eagle	1, .5, .25, .1 oz.	1997 - present	Limited Edition Proof Coins Sold at Numismatic Premiums

Country	Name of Coin	Sizes	Issue Date(s)	Comments
Armenia	Centenary	1 oz.	1990	"Coins of Tradition"
Australia	Proof Koala	1, .5, .25, .1, .05 oz.	1988 - Present	5 Coin Set
Bophuthatswana	President L.M. Mangope	1 oz.	1987	Set
Canada	Sea Otter	1, .5, .25, .1 oz.	1994	
Canada	Cougar	1, .5, .25, .1 oz.	1992	Set
Canada	Owl	1, .5, .25, .1 oz.	1991	Set
Canada	Polar Bear	1, .5, .25, .1 oz.	1990	4 coin set
Canada	Proof Maple Leaf	1, .5, .25, .1 oz.	1989	4 Coin Set honoring 10th anniversary of PML
China	Invention and Discovery series	1 oz.,	1993 - Present	5 coin set
China	Lunar Zodiac Series	Listed below		
	Ram	1 oz.	1991	
	Horse	1 oz.	1990	
	Snake	1 oz.	1989	
	Dragon	1 oz.	1988	
China	Panda	1 oz.	1987 - 1990	
Dominican Republic	500th Anniversary/ Discovery of America	15.55g (.5 oz.)	1990 - 1992	
France	Louvre 200th Anniversary Series	Listed Below		
	Mona Lisa	1 oz.	1994 - Present	
	Venus De Milo	1 oz.	1994 - Present	
	Liberte' (De La Croix)	17 grams	1994 - Present	
	Victoria de Sr. Samothrace	17 grams	1994 - Present	
	Napoleon (David)	17 grams	1994 - Present	
	Marguerite	17 grams	1994 - Present	
France	Descartes	20 grams (.6431 oz.)	1991	
France	Eiffel Tower	16 grams (.5145 oz.)	1989	5 Francs
France	Bicentennial of French Revolution Series	Listed below		100 Francs
	Rights of Man (Human Rights)	20 grams (.6431 oz.)	1989	

Country	Name of Coin	Sizes	Issue Date(s)	Comments
	Fraternity	20 grams (.6431 oz.)	1988	
	Equality - Marquis de Lafayette	20 grams (.6431 oz.)	1987	
	Liberty - Statue of Liberty	20 grams (.6431 oz.)	1986	
France	Lafayette	20 grams (.6431 oz.)	1987	
Gibraltar	Christmas	30.4 grams (.9775 oz.)	1988 - Present	
Gibraltar	500th Anniversary of Columbus	18 grams (.5788 oz.)	1992	
Gibraltar	Olympic Series	.2 oz	1992	Eight design types
Gibraltar	Soccer	.2 oz.	1990	
Isle of Man	Noble - proof	.2 oz.	1983 - Present	
Isle of Man	Persian Cat	1, .5, .2, .1 oz.	1989 - Present	
Isle of Man	Christmas	.9286 oz.	1980 - Present	30.4 grams total
Isle of Man	150th Anniversay of "Penny Black" Stamp	1.5884 oz.	1990	
Isle of Man	Queen Mother Theme	.2 oz.	1990	6.22 grams total
Isle of Man	World Cup - Italy	1.5884 oz.	1990	
Isle of Man	Bicentenary of US Constitution	1 oz.	1987	
Isle of Man	Prince Andrew's Wedding	1.5884 oz. (52 grams)	1986	
Isle of Man	World Cup - Mexico	1.5884 oz. (52 grams)	1986	
Isle of Man	30th Commonwealth Parliamentary Conference	1.5884 oz. (52 grams)	1984	
Isle of Man	Quincentenary of the College of Arms	1.5884 oz. (52 grams)	1984	
Isle of Man	1984 Olympics - Sarajevo, Los Angeles	1.5884 oz. (52 grams)	1984	
Isle of Man	Tourist Trophy Motorcycle Races	.9286 oz.	1981 - 1984	

Country	Name of Coin	Sizes	Issue Date(s)	Comments
Isle of Man	Bicentenary of Manned Flight	1.5884 oz. (52 grams)	1983	
Isle of Man	World Cup - Spain	1.5884 oz. (52 grams)	1982	
Isle of Man	Manx Maritime Heritage	1.5884 oz. (52 grams)	1982	
Isle of Man	Duke of Edinburgh	1.5884 oz. (52 grams)	1981	
Isle of Man	International Year of the Disabled	1.5884 oz. (52 grams)	1981	
Isle of Man	Wedding of Prince Charles and Lady Diana	1.5884 oz. (52 grams)	1981	
Isle of Man	Bicentenary of the Derby	1.5884 oz. (52 grams)	1980	
Isle of Man	1980 Olympics - Lake Placid, Moscow	1.5884 oz. (52 grams)	1980	
Isle of Man	Millennium of Tynwald	1.5884 oz. (52 grams)	1979	
Isle of Man	Pence Series			Various denominations - legal tender proof coins
Italy	"Europa 1993"	15.5g, 31.1g	1993 - Present	Combination platinum and gold coin
Mexico	Rainbow	1, .5, .25 oz., (1989 Pt.= .25 oz., 1990 Pt.=1 oz, 1991 Pt.= .5 oz.)	1989 - 1991	Platinum, Silver, Gold - Set Rotates
Mexico	1/4 Onza	.25 oz.	1989	
Panama	Champions of Boxing	.2940 oz. (9.33 grams)	1980	
Panama	150th Anniversary, Pan-American Congress	.2987 oz. (9.3 grams)	1976	
Panama	Balboa	Listed Below		
	150th Anniversary Pan-American Congress	9.3g (.2987 oz.)	1976	
	Panama Canal Treaty Implementation	9.5g (.2994 oz.)	1979	

Country	Name of Coin	Sizes	Issue Date(s)	Comments
Panama	Champions of Boxing	9.33g (.2940 oz.)	1980	
Papua New Guinea	Butterfly	.3061 oz. (9.57 grams)	1992	
Portugal	Discovery Series			10 sets over 12 years (2 completed so far) 4 metal sets - platinum, palladium, gold, silver
Singapore	25 Years of Independence	1 oz.	1990	4 coins and a bank note
Switzerland	Helvetias	1, .5, .25, .1 oz.	1987	
Switzerland	Shooting Taler	1 oz.	1986, 1987	
Tonga	Seven Sided Christmas		1982	
Russia	Ballerina Proof	.5, .25, .1 oz.	1994 - Present	Set
Russia	Historical Collection 1, 2	Listed below		
	"Battaglia Di Chemsma" (Italian)	15.55 grams	1992	
	War of Liberation vs. Napoleon	.5 oz.	1991	(6th in series)
	The Patriotic War of 1812	.5 oz.	1991	150 ruble face value
	Ship St. Gavriil	.5 oz.	1990	
	Battle of Poltava River	.5 oz.	1990	
	Glasnost	.5 oz.	1989	
	Nicholas II	1 oz.	1989	
	Encounter on the Ungra River	.5 oz.	1989	Depicts battle between Ivan III and the Mongols
	1000 Years of Literature	.5 oz.	1988	
	Grand Duke Igor	.5 oz.	1988	
USSR	Olympic Series	15.54 grams	1977 - 1980	
USA	Eagle	1, .5, .25, .1oz.	First year of issue: 1997	Reverse changes annually.
Venezuela	General Gomez	1.31 oz. (40.9 grams)		(Munich Mint)

Palladium Coins

Country	Name of Coin	Sizes	Issue Date(s)	Comments
Armenia	Centenary	1 oz.	1990	
Bermuda	Wreck of the "San Antonio"	1 oz	1988	British Royal Mint
Bermuda	"Sea Venture" Sailing Ship	1 oz.	1987	
China	Panda	1 oz.	1989	
France	Lafayette	17 grams	1987	Total weight 17 grams, 90% palladium 10% silver
France	Bicentennial of French Revolution	12 grams	1988	10 Francs face value
Isle of Man	Americas Cup	1 oz.	1987	
Isle of Man	Bicentenary of US Constitution	1 oz.	1987	
Latvia	Latvian Historic Battleship	1 oz.	1989	
Portugal	Discovery Series			10 sets over 12 years (2 completed so far) 4 metal sets - platinum, palladium, gold, silver 4 coin set
Tonga	Americas Cup	1 oz.	1987	
Russia	Ballerina	1, .5, .25 oz.	1989, 1990, 1994 - Present	(proof and bullion)
Russia	Historical Collection 1,2	Listed below		
	Catherine II	1 oz.	1992	
	Abolition of Serfdom 1861	1 oz.	1991	25 ruble face value
	Peter the Great	1 oz.	1990	
	Ivan III - Founder of Russian State	1 oz.	1989	
	St. Vladimir, Grand Duke of Kiev	1 oz.	1988	
	Millennium of Christianity	.5 oz.	1988	
Switzerland	Shooting Taler	1 oz.	1990	

The Rarest of
Earth Metals for
Your Rare Coin Retirement

By all accounts, platinum and palladium are among the rarest of earth metals that have in their family gold and other precious metal products. Like their siblings, they are highly collectible and have a rich numismatic past and present.

Platinum in particular has a significant price gain, rising from $359 in January, 1997 to more than $430 in October, 1997, a $70 per ounce price change, equal to about 20 percent annually. The price fell to $359.10 on December 24, 1997, but by January 14, 1998, it was up to $386. Yet, even with the mild changes, both up and down, the price change has been steady, a pleasing contrast to the wild fluctuations of the Dow Jones Industrial Average, whose height is about a 22 percent gain, but whose downside is substantially different—even after its spectacular 500 point drop on October 27. Early 1998 was not materially better, with the overall Dow fluctuating 3 percent over the course of just a week.

Congress has given recognition to platinum, gold and silver as prime investment vehicles with the 1997 tax law that grants American eagle bullion coins the same favorable capital gains treatment as stocks and bonds.

One result of this is that it has been legal since the first of the year to include platinum eagles in your individual retirement accounts as well as self-directed plans. Gold and silver eagles also can presently be put in into the plans. These coins can also be put

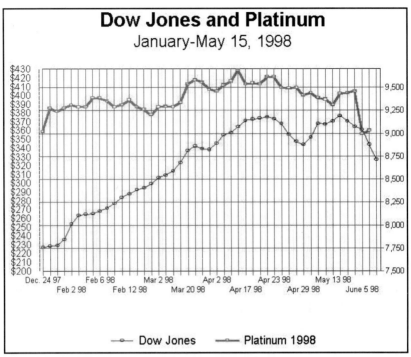

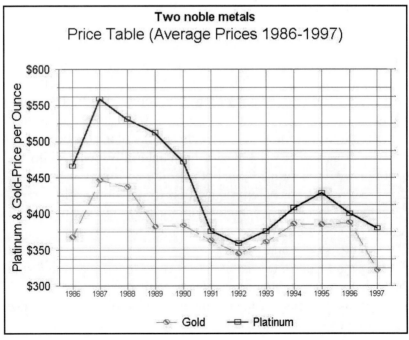

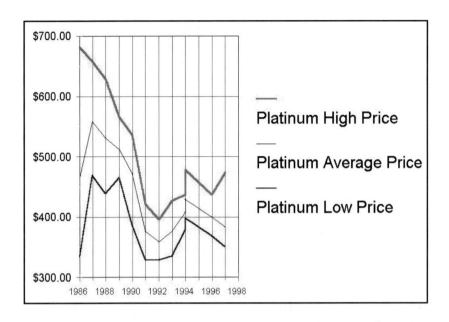

——	**Platinum High Price**
——	**Platinum Average Price**
——	**Platinum Low Price**

into old fashioned IRA accounts that allow for tax-deferred income gains, or into the new Roth-IRA that puts in already taxed income, but permits withdrawals tax free (including the gains) after you reach age 59.5.

Alan Greenspan, the chairman of the Federal Reserve, has repeatedly said that the stock market is flying too high. When he did it in April, the Dow Jones Industrial Average fell more than 500 points as if to fulfill the prophecy, thanks in part to the Fed's decision to raise interest rates.

Bullion prices for gold, silver and platinum by contrast have an almost contrary attitude—far more reflective of traditional supply and demand requirements of the economy than before, with a result that prices are much higher.

Since March 10, 1997, approaching what stock market analysts call a "technical correction," of 10 percent, but what private investors are heard to call a disaster, the market has gone from nearly 7100 to interday trading of below 6500, to 8000, back into the 6000 range, and then to more than 8000 again, all in a ten month period of time. And, after a 300 point drop on October 23 and 24 that correlated with the changes in the Japanese and Hong Kong markets, there was a further spectacular fall October 27 as the bottom appeared to drop out of the market when it fell to 7300, a 500 point drop (the largest in history).

The swing after the first of the new year has been as dramatic, and as calamitous for the small investor. Institutional investors, however, seem to make out well in these tumultuous times.

To those who remember the time when the Dow moved 10 points it was big financial news, often on the front page of a daily newspaper, it is simply unfathomable that 100 point gains are now almost a yawnfest. It's about the same as a space trip to the moon; what was once front page news is now barely a mention on the wire services.

But look at the numbers. At the start of last year, the Dow stood at around 6560. It rose readily peaking at 7078 on March 10 —a gain of about 7.9 percent over three months (annualized to more than 31 percent). It then rose to more than 8000, fell, only to rise again. Gains as of mid-October were about 23 percent on the year. By year's end, it rose, fell, and rose again in a Santa Claus rally.

Strictly as a contrast, here's how precious metal prices began 1997—for platinum, gold, and silver all as reported by Kitco Minerals & Metals Inc. Consider it at various mileposts throughout the year.

	Gold	Platinum	Silver
Jan 6 97	359.25	362.75	4.66
Mar 3	361.80	390.50	5.31
May 1	339.55	372.25	4.68
Aug 1	325.30	436.50	4.64
Oct 10	327.00	430.00	5.14
Oct 22	322.00	419.00	4.97
Oct 27	311.00	413.00	4.82
Dec 24	296.00	359.10	6.26
Jan 6 98	281.50	358.00	6.02
Jan 14 98	285.90	386.00	5.70

Platinum, which started 1997 at around $360 an ounce (and presently is at $386 an ounce) is not immune to the general financial activities, and moved in tandem with the expanding economy into the $384 range, to $413 and beyond, before slowly giving back some of the profits as the Dow shrank still further, expanding again as the Dow rose.

There were sound reasons for the platinum change, some of which can be explained by its use as an industrial metal that just happens to be precious. In addition, Russian platinum exports (which comprise 20 percent of world platinum) have been shut down awaiting a parliamentary decision as to how much can be exported. (Exports in 1997 of platinum, palladium and unfinished gems from the Russian state were substantial. Gokhran, the state fund for precious stones and metals, said it sold 13 billion rubles ($217 million) of rough gems and platinum group metals to help pay off state debts to workers).

But as the accompanying graph shows, platinum evidenced considerable resilience, opening a wide gap with gold (and moving to a 20 percent premium or more over the spot price of gold) while also doing better, at least on a trend line, than the Dow.

Gold's drop is all but inexplicable, ridiculously dropping below $285 an ounce, even as inflation mocks the decline with its worst showing in a generation—a mere 1.7 percent annual increase according to government statistics.

There appear to be a number of reasons for the price change. One may be the increased availability of platinum as a metal in the American market, thanks to the decision last year to create a platinum bullion coin. Another may also have to do with the decision of some mining authorities to withhold platinum from the marketplace, at the same time that gold bullion has been dumped, not at fire sale prices, but certainly in a manner that is depressing to the overall market.

The CPM Group theorizes that industrial demand for platinum has expanded by 5 percent this year, at a time when the Russian government's exports have been reduced by about 10 percent—more than enough to impact the overall marketplace.

This analysis precedes the U.S. government's entry into the bullion platinum business, which is selling briskly, and the proof platinum program, which has sold an unexpectedly high 30,000 ounces and gone to a near sell-out. In fact, platinum sales by the U.S. have been far from a statistical anomaly or even modest; more than 100,000 troy ounces of the metal were sold during the first six months of the program.

The platinum bullion program is expected to be shaped differently from that of the other bullion programs for gold and silver because the designs on at least one side of the coin will change each year. Mint officials have learned from the past mistakes associated with other bullion and proof precious metal coin ventures. The platinum program is legislatively designed in a way that is to grant maximum marketing opportunities and efforts to the mint, rather than Congress.

Issuance of the new platinum bullion coins was not done in a vacuum, nor is it the first contemporary authorization of a platinum coin. Congress authorized the Smithsonian commemorative coin program produced in 1996 to have a platinum component, or to use a more traditional gold coin. Treasury Secretary Rubin elected to use a gold $5 coin, and did not experiment with a platinum issue. But all the while the mint and the Treasury were planning on the issuance of a major bullion program.

Platinum's current journey to become the sixth metal to be utilized as a major component of coin manufacturing (the others are copper, nickel, zinc, gold and silver) began a little over two years ago when legislation was introduced in the House of Representatives to create a platinum bullion coin. Credit for this goes to Congressman John Olver, D-Mass.

Initially, the legislation was extensive and precise as to what should be produced, how it should be manufactured, the design that it should contain, and the other elements that Congress has historically assigned to coins over the last 208 years.

The legislation moved nowhere, partly because Olver was relatively low on seniority, and, by 1994, a member of the minority party. The other reason is that there was no particular outside interest for or against the proposal.

Olver's legislation was simply one of 20,000 bills that are introduced each year in Congress, of which only about 600 become law.

Things took a boost when Rep. Michael Castle, R-Del., chairman of the House coinage subcommittee, introduced legislation designed to reform the commemorative coinage system and also to authorize manufacturing of platinum commemorative coinage.

The Treasury Secretary Decides

Though his bill's language gave the secretary of the Treasury power to determine design, there were certain specific elements that were required under the law. Among them:

"On each coin minted under this subsection, there shall be—(A) a designation of the value of the coin and the weight of the platinum content of the coin; (B) an inscription of the year in which the coin is minted or issued; and (C) inscriptions of the words 'Liberty,' 'In God We Trust,' 'United States of America,' and 'E Pluribus Unum.' "

Castle's legislation came after a year of holding hearings on various infirmities in the commemorative coinage system, and after having opted to show the mint that he was interested in a platinum alternative with the Smithsonian commemorative.

This initiative passed the House of Representatives on a voice vote, whereupon it was presented to the Senate for consideration. There it sat, legislation without a sponsor or voice to carry the day.

Still, it had powerful friends, principally Sen. Alphonse D'Amato, R-N.Y., chairman of the Senate Banking Committee, who took an interest in the measure—and ultimately agreed to insert it as a rider to unrelated legislation.

What finally emerged was legislation that was appended to the Treasury, Postal Service and General Government Appropriations Bill of 1997, legislation that was literally passed on the final day before the government would have had to shut down for the third or fourth time in this session of Congress.

Instead, amidst hundreds of pages of authorizations for various governmental programs such as Internal Revenue Service tax collection, and delivery of the mail, an obscure provision was inserted based on near-unanimous agreement of the Senate and House.

"The Secretary may mint and issue bullion and proof platinum coins in accordance with such specifications, designs, varieties, quantities, denominations and inscriptions as the Secretary, in the Secretary's discretion, may prescribe from time to time."

With these words, and an incantation that also allowed the Treasury secretary to produce gold bullion coins both in their traditional 22 karat (.900 fine) mode and in 24 karat (.9999 fine) gold, American coinage law was significantly changed.

Part of the reason for the effort is the revenue that the platinum and virtually pure gold coins will bring. A joint Senate-House Conference Report on the appropriations bill reports that, "Receipts from the sales of these additional programs is estimated at $21,100,000 in 1997 and $88,900,000 over five years and will be deposited into the General Fund of the Treasury for deficit reduction."

The United States finally entered the era of platinum coinage May 1, 1997 with the historic first strike ceremony at its newest mint (West Point) located in an equally historic setting (the United States Military Academy). The first issue was a $100 coin dated 1997, containing just a tad over 1 troy ounce of the precious metal.

Philip N. Diehl, the 35th director of the United States Mint, used both hands to simultaneously push large buttons on each side of the large Grabener hydraulic press at a few minutes after eleven o'clock in the morning on May 1.

By holding them down, he completed the electrical circuit to the die on the press. That then caused 120 metric tons of pressure to strike a hand-fed blank platinum planchet, placed their moments before by press operator Elena Citron.

"Woosh," followed by a deadened thud, masked by a thick lucite plate coming between the die and the exterior bed of the press was all that was initially heard. This was closely followed by eight more thuds programmed into the computerized press.

The one ounce platinum proof coin was struck a total of

nine times—the most ever utilized for a large-issue striking program that will require each blank to be hand-fed into the press,
and individually removed by the operator.

In the mint's history dating back to 1792, only one other
coin has taken a total of nine strikes to bring up the design—the
fabled Ultra High Relief $20 gold pieces of 1907, struck with 172
tons of pressure with nine blows.

That was for a circulation strike, however, and the con-
straints of production needs eventually precluded using so many
blows on a hydraulic press intended for medals, and not for coin
of the realm—and thus the relief was lowered for the regular issues.

Double striking of proof coins is not unusual either, and
the second strike typically fleshes out the metal flow and brings a
razor-sharp rim and extraordinary design detail that collectors
have come to prize. But working gold, and other metals, is different from platinum, which is dense and not as ductile. The result:
to obtain the proof relief that collectors so prize, at least six strikes
are required; the seventh through ninth strikes bring out intricate
design details of John Mercanti's *Portrait of Liberty* and Thomas
Rogers, Sr.'s *Soaring Bald Eagle.*

"The eagle soars!" Diehl declared as press operator Citron
used tongs to present him with the new platinum eagle coin that
he then held aloft. He examined the obverse and reverse, and then
held up the coin for the assembled to see.

This was the smallest first strike ceremony ever conducted
at the West Point Mint, which was originally created in 1937 as a
United States Bullion Depositary, to hold the nation's silver reserves. Two bullion depositories were simultaneously constructed:
one at Fort Knox, Kentucky, on the military reservation of the
United States Army Armor Center, the other at the United States
Military Academy at West Point, New York.

Pressed into service as a minting facility that was adjunct
to Philadelphia in the mid 1970s because of a shortage of one cent
coinage, it became the premiere minting facility for U.S. precious
metal coinage precisely because of the security that was built in to
watch the nation's bullion supply. Both Fort Knox and West Point

have a distinctive feature: the building itself is a giant vault, and inside the building is a vault within the vault, where the precious metal is stored. At West Point, that is where a small production area has been constructed complete with the latest technology and world-class coining presses.

Platinum used in the coinage is .9995 fine. The one ounce coin produced has a diameter of 32.7mm in size, about 2mm larger in size than a standard half dollar, and a thickness a bit over a tenth of an inch. All of the metal presently comes from three sources: Johnson-Matthey, Englehardt Industries, and Tanaka (Tokyo). The mint purchases pre-made blanks that are already upset, that is, rimmed and ready for striking.

Every eighteen strikes—two coins for the proof mintages— the press operator took out a special cloth and poured lubrication fluid before cleaning the die. Estimated die life is between 550 and 600 coins for the proof coins (about 5,000 strikes).

A maximum of 21,000 of the one ounce pieces are slated for the first year of issue. Also scheduled for production as a proof: half ounce (18,000 maximum mintage), quarter ounce (23,000 maximum mintage) and tenth ounce (38,000 maximum) coins.

The weights and values are correlated such that the tenth ounce is a tenth of $100 or $10; the half ounce and quarter ounce also follow logically. Gold bullion issues use $5, $10, $25 and $50 for the face value of comparably-weighted precious metal.

A total of 8,000 of the one ounce coins are reserved for a four coin proof set (tenth, quarter, half and ounce) that will have a retail selling price of $1,350. Another 5,000 pieces are reserved for a set of gold, silver and platinum ounces, which has a prospective price of $1,499.

That means that only 8,000 of the one ounce pieces will be available for sale, individually, at a price of $695 apiece. The half ounce proof will carry a price of $395, the quarter ounce $199 and the tenth of an ounce $99. (The combined price is a $28 savings over individual prices).

The tenth of an ounce proof requires two strikes from the Grabener press working at fifty tons of pressure; the quarter ounce takes three swipes at seventy tons of pressure. The half ounce also takes as many as nine strikes at 100 tons to bring the 27mm diameter coin up to snuff.

Orders will be accepted by the mint if postmarked on or after June 6, and the coins will be marketed through the end of the year, unless they sell out first—which mint officials believe is very possible and highly probable.

The proof coins are a prelude to the introduction of a bullion coin program for platinum that will also start later this year. Those coins will be struck twice to achieve an attractive design for the Statue of Liberty obverse and soaring eagle reverse.

With this program, the United States joins a number of other countries who produce platinum, gold, and silver bullion programs, as well as a comparable proof coin that is intended for collectors.

At a Los Angeles premiere held for the purpose of launching the platinum coin program to the public at large, Philip Diehl, U.S. Mint director, seemed very pleased with progress to date, measured against the mint's expectations, not those of some critics.

So did Jacques Luben, executive director of the Platinum Guild, an industry trade organization that has been instrumental in the promotion not only of platinum as an investment vehicle, but also as an American coin standard.

That proved in the first year to be successful with a virtual sell out on the proof issues, a secondary market at higher than expected levels for the quarter and half ounce bullion and numismatic items, and keener interest and higher prices.

No one knows where any precious metal is going to go, but what seems clear enough is that the future of the new American platinum bullion coin is a bright one, and the proof platinum issues could be just about the best new investment product to come down the road in along time. The same is true of the contemporary issues from many foreign countries.